Swimming in the American:

A Memoir and Selected Writings

by

Hiroshi Kashiwagi

Asian American Curriculum Project
San Mateo, California

SWIMMING IN THE AMERICAN:
A MEMOIR AND SELECTED WRITINGS
Copyright © 2005 by Hiroshi Kashiwagi
With the exception of the photographs listed below,
all images are courtesy of the author.

Published in the United States by the
Asian American Curriculum Project (AACP)
P.O. Box 1587, San Mateo, CA 94401
529 East Third Avenue, San Mateo, CA 94401
Tel: (800) 874-2242
Fax: (650) 357-6908
Printed in Canada

Edited by Tamiko F. Nimura

Cover photography:
Front cover, background:
American River, Sacramento, CA *(Josh Parmenter)*
Front cover, inserts, left to right:
Fukumatsu Kashiwagi and Kashiwagi family
(courtesy of Hiroshi Kashiwagi);
Tule Lake guard tower *(Jack Iwata,
National Archives, courtesy of National
Japanese American Historical Society (NJAHS))*;
Japanese Americans volunteering for the U.S. Army
(Toyo Miyatake, courtesy of NJAHS);
Tule Lake arrivals *(John Bigelow, courtesy of NJAHS)*;
Hiroshi Kashiwagi in "Nativity Cycle," UC Berkeley
(courtesy of Hiroshi Kashiwagi);
Hiroshi Kashiwagi testifying before the Commission
on Wartime Relocation, San Francisco, CA, 1981
(Isao Isago Tanaka, courtesy of NJAHS)

Book design by Pamela Matsuoka

Library of Congress Control Number: 2004117432
Non-Fiction • 5.5" x 8.25" • 252 pages
$14.95 • ISBN 0-934609-15-2

Dedication

*To the memory of Wayne M. Collins
who rescued me as an American and
restored my faith in America.*

Funding for this library edition
made possible by the
**Henri and Tomoye Takahashi
Charitable Foundation**
⌘
Asian American Curriculum Project
⌘
Hiroshi Kashiwagi

ACKNOWLEDGMENTS

I am fortunate to have a talented niece, Tamiko Nimura, who edited the manuscript and gave me so much support in the preparation of this book. Her husband Josh Parmenter assisted me with the computer work, which was more help than I like to admit. He also took the photograph of the American River which is part of the book cover.

I want to thank my family—my wife Sadako for her unfailing love and support; our children Tosh, Soji and his wife Keiko, and Hiroshi F. for always being on my side and for being such great human beings.

I also acknowledge my friends who have been important in my life—Ted and Lee Samuel, theater folks I've known for over half a century; Jim Hirabayashi, fellow actor and nisei cohort; and the late artist Gompers Saijo whom I had asked to design the book cover but sadly it wasn't meant to be.

I would like to give credit to the late Michi Weglyn, whose pioneering work, *Years of Infamy*, William Morrow and Company, Inc., New York, 1976, was a constant source of inspiration.

I am grateful for the California Civil Liberties Public Education Program grant which made possible this publication. I want to acknowledge Kevin Starr, the former State Librarian and Diane Matsuda who were responsible for this educational program which enabled the Japanese Americans to tell their stories, especially of their incarceration experience during world War II.

I also would like to thank Pamela Matsuoka, graphic designer, and Florence Hongo and Philip Chin of the Asian American Curriculum Project for publishing this book.

Preface

This book is about my life, from my birth to the present. The format is essentially chronological covering my childhood years of the twenties, the Great Depression years of the thirties, the World War II years of the forties, and the postwar years to the present. However, it is not a straight narrative because it is a collection of vignettes that highlight certain events and moments of my life. These pieces were originally written at different points in my life, covering timely events or recollecting events of the past. So the chronology is sometimes blurred, the time jumping back and forth like flashbacks within a flashback. Through this "cinematic" method I hope to achieve a kind of impressionistic whole of my life story. Included also are poems which add a different perspective. Life wasn't always grim; there was some levity that leavened the days.

—*Hiroshi Kashiwagi*

Table of Contents

Dog Story

According to the Asian zodiac, the year I was born, 1922, was the year of the dog. There are two dogs that were a big part of my boyhood: Prince, who I'll write about later, and Spot, the dog I made up.

When we were in the sixth grade, always on Monday, the teacher would have us get up in front of the class and talk about what we did over the weekend. It was bad enough going back to school on Monday but the thought of the story hour made me miserable. Nothing made me feel more inadequate. The problem was I had nothing to tell. This, I later discovered, was the crux of the problem. One must have something to say, something that one feels confident with; otherwise, one will be a nervous wreck, as I was every Monday.

But I was home all weekend, because I usually helped in the store. I didn't think to talk about that; it was too commonplace, I had been doing that since I was seven years old. Sometimes I played with my brother and sister but, being older, I was never part of their games. I didn't like playing cars as they did endlessly, crawling on their hands and knees, making car noises and pushing their little cars, usually made out of wooden blocks.

I didn't go anywhere either. Occasionally we visited our friends in the country for a soak in their Japanese tub—but who would want to hear about that. Although it was special for us, especially for our parents, things Japanese like ofuro (tub bath) or zori (go ahead slippers) or tofu or sushi, I tried to keep to myself, afraid that others would find them strange and even laughable. Was I ashamed of my Japanese background? I don't know. It is a source of amazement to me that all those Japanese things have become familiar if not commonplace in American culture. We never wore zori during the day unless we were sick in bed but now people wear them everywhere, day or night, indoors or out.

Nothing really happened to me, not in the way things happened to others. They always had plenty to tell—they had parties, received gifts, gone on trips, visited friends and relatives. One boy in the class had four aunts with whom he visited every weekend or did something with each in turn. So he never ran out of stories. How lucky for him—and unfair for me. Where were my relatives? Did I have any at all? Maybe in Japan, but certainly none close by. Some boys told about going fishing or hunting which was boring to me; obviously, I had never gone fishing or hunting and I never believed their stories but they seemed to fascinate everyone. People listened to them. Why couldn't I tell a hunting story? But I never went hunting.

One Monday morning when my turn came around, I went up front. Strangely, I felt quite confident as I began, "Over the weekend I went hunting with my dog Spot." I had never held a gun in my hand, much less shot one, but I had the kids' rapt attention. No one had ever heard of Spot either. He was an invention. I remembered the pasture on the ranch where we had lived before we moved to town. That was where I set the story; I could picture the blackberry bush. I continued, "Spot went on ahead and I followed. Then I saw something move in the bush and thinking it was a rabbit, I fired. When I heard a yelp, I ran to look and found that I had shot my dog Spot." I thought I heard a gasp.

That was my story—short, simple, uncomplicated, straightforward and completely fictitious.

As I walked back to my seat, the kids looked at me strangely;

they couldn't quite believe what they had heard, yet it was shocking enough that they didn't dare question it.

Of course, I didn't let on that I had made it up. After a moment, the teacher said, "Sometimes accidents like that happen; we must be very careful when we go hunting."

After that I had no problem with the story hour. With a little fabrication, I learned, I could tell an interesting story that would hold the kids' attention. I was relaxed and I began to enjoy the other stories, appreciate them more. I had a feeling some of them were fabrications too.

<u>Beginning</u>

I was born in a boarding house in Sacramento on November 8, 1922, delivered by a midwife to whom I am grateful for bringing me into the world. Apparently, it was a very normal birth. Obviously, I did not know or meet the midwife, but I think she was from Kumamoto Prefecture in southern Japan. My theory of her origin is that when she registered my birth she gave our family name as "Kashiwaki," the way folks from Kumamoto would pronounce the name instead of the usual "Kashiwagi." It was a natural thing for her to do. I am familiar with the Kumamoto dialect because, growing up, I heard it spoken by our customers, many of whom were from Kumamoto.

No one was aware of this discrepancy until the outbreak of World War II when we had to take a hard look at our birth certificates. Mother, though embarrassed, could not explain the error, which, as far as I was concerned, invalidated the document. So I wrote to the Bureau of Vital Statistics in Sacramento to make the correction. In the process I found a friend in Mr. Flynn, the kind postmaster and notary public of Penryn, who notarized the necessary documents in making the change. He was so patient and understanding that I feel he was genuinely concerned for me in correcting my birth name.

When I was born, my parents were living in Florin. They

were a part of a small colony of Japanese engaged in growing strawberries. Though I was an infant and wasn't aware, Florin was a segregated town with a separate school for non-white children who were mainly Chinese and Japanese. I guess the so-called "Oriental" parents did not question this, thinking it was the way things were in America. Florin was only a few miles from Sacramento, but of course the capital was teeming with anti-Oriental politicians of the time.

Our immigrant parents wanted, above all else, to live peaceably, especially with their Caucasian bosses and neighbors. They would not think of complaining and causing trouble—and besides, the school was good with excellent hakujin (white) teachers. The children would get a good education, learn English, and become good citizens. The school remained segregated until the fall of 1941 when the local Japanese American Citizens League succeeded in their efforts to integrate the schools. Ironically, this happened just before Pearl Harbor and our subsequent removal to the camps.

I'm glad we did not settle in Florin permanently. When I was a year old, the family moved to Walnut Grove where father tried in vain to make a living fishing for striped bass in the lower Sacramento River. Walnut Grove was settled originally by both Japanese and Chinese immigrants, though the Chinese later found the town of Locke which was near Walnut Grove.

Mother, who was quite idle, would take me out on the boardwalk every day—she became known as the attractive but destitute young mother with her little boy. Poor thing, where was her husband? Out fishing? Does he catch any fish? Does he bring any home to eat, much less to sell? She better have a talk with him. The people would shake their heads. Fishing was poor and it was foolish for anyone to try to make a living from it. Everyone in town knew that except father, who refused to give up his dream. Although still a young bride, this was when mother realized she had married a stubborn and hard-headed man, and that unless she asserted herself, she and the family would suffer. She challenged

KOFUSA KASHIWAGI (20), HIROSHI (1). (CA 1923)

him then and apparently won—at what cost I don't know—but we soon moved back to the boarding house in Sacramento.

Through the years mother's assertiveness and kindred stubbornness would result in many arguments and frightening scenes, so frightening that we children would start crying, especially when father threatened to beat mother. Sometimes he did. There is an early family portrait in which mother claims her face is swollen—the night before the picture was taken, father had slapped her during an argument. Swollen face or not, mother still looks beautiful. What was most scary was when father sometimes angrily splashed water on mother, a symbolic act that barely masked his anger and violence but was more frightening than the actual blow to her face or head. Seeing mother, humiliated and helpless, brushing away the water from her face, made me want to cry all the more. But she always held her ground.

Mother and I stayed at the boarding house while father found work in the fruit orchards in the neighboring towns. My brother and sister were born during this period. The boarding house was to be our temporary home until we settled more or less permanently in Loomis, about twenty five miles east of Sacramento in the foothills. Early immigrants from England, Germany and Denmark had settled there and had cleared the land for fruit orchards. They were now renting the farms to the Japanese or sharecropping with them.

The window from our second story room in the boarding house faced "I" Street. We were warned not to get too close to the window for fear of falling out, as a child had done earlier. A horse-drawn ice cream wagon with its tinkling bell came to tempt us several times a day. A tobacco shop on the corner had a revolving display of chewing gum that always fascinated me.

We were one of a few families in the house. I believe father was related to the owner of the boarding house. Most of the boarders were single men, transients between jobs. They would come up from their cold, damp rooms in the basement, often coughing and spitting. Conditions were not exactly hygienic—we all ate at the same table and shared the communal bath. As I write this, I realize that this might have been the source of the tuberculosis that plagued us later. Several members of the family that ran the boarding house would also be afflicted with TB and eventually succumb to it.

The prawns in their shells, cooked in sweet soy sauce, were a frequent lunch or dinner fare. Apparently this was a popular boarding house dish, as prawns in those days were plentiful and cheap and easy for the cook to prepare in large quantities. Though adults seemed to relish the dish, I thought it was a lot of trouble shelling the prawns for a little bit of food. (To this day, I prefer seafood that's already shelled.) Sometimes a Chinese waiter from a nearby restaurant came with a covered platter of chow mein hoisted above his shoulder. He always made it a special occasion for me. I don't recall eating the chow mein, only the tantalizing smell which I later learned was the bean spouts still cooking, and the waiter at whom I marveled. Even now I am fascinated by the sight of waiters in restaurants marching in with platters held above their shoulder.

Most of the orchards in Loomis were ten to twenty acres of plum and peach trees with a small pasture and barn for the horses used for plowing and draying. A packing shed, a cabin, an outhouse, and a bathhouse completed the layout for the tenant. Sometimes, there was a well in place of running water. Usually on higher ground was the owner's home: a two-story house, often painted white with inside plumbing, and a large yard with huge shady trees and a sloping lawn. The house always seemed cool even in the hottest of summer days. There was a distinct smell that emanated from the house. Japanese called it "butter smell." I don't know where they got that; it was a unique smell that I used to regard as "hakujin" or white folk's smell. It might have been from the butter they used in cooking, which we Japanese never did. But I always liked butter spread on bread.

Kindergarten

very morning mother would fill my lunch with a meat sandwich, a large piece of cake or cookies, and a banana or an apple. It was a wonderful lunch—if only I didn't have to go to kindergarten with it.

"Don't forget your Obento," mother would remind me. Once I had forgotten to take my lunch and father had to make a special trip bringing it to school.

At kindergarten I put my lunch pail in the cloakroom. The lavatory was in another building a short distance away.

Everything about kindergarten was foreign to me. Miss Grace, our teacher, came to school riding a horse. She was always in boots and riding habit and usually wore a big hat. She was the tallest woman I had ever seen. After hitching the horse to a tree, she came into the classroom.

"Good Morning, children," Miss Grace always greeted us cheerfully.

"Good Morning, Miss Grace," we children said in unison.

The children all spoke English, which I didn't understand. I knew only Japanese then.

The class began every morning with the Pledge of Allegiance to the flag. Then we sang "America." Miss Grace accompanied us loudly on the upright piano.

Miss Grace taught us English. She told stories and read from a book. We also drew pictures and played with clay. For some reason, everything I made with clay turned into snakes.

During recess the children ran outside to play on the slide and the swing. I didn't make any friends. The girls were off by themselves and the rough-and-tumble boys were frightening.

One day the boys discovered my lunch. Then everyday at lunchtime they crowded around me to pick on all the good things that mother had packed in my lunch pail. They fought like little animals.

My parents thought everything was fine at kindergarten. They thought I was having a good time, learning English and about America and making new friends. I didn't tell them what was happening to my lunch and how miserable I was.

One day I ran home from school. As soon as father let me off the Model T Ford and drove off, I started for home. It was about three miles on the country road but I took shortcuts. In my hurry, I barely noticed the cows and horses grazing in the pasture, the poppies and the lupines blooming in the fields, and the plum trees in the orchards, already green with leaves. Actually, it was a beautiful late spring day in the Sierra foothills.

I was home before father drove up and mother was puzzled. She had seen me come home.

"I thought you took him to kindergarten," she asked.

"Yes, I did," father said, "I left him at school before I went into town."

"But he's home."

"What?"

I was certain I would be scolded, even whipped. But father began to laugh and mother joined him, so I laughed too. We all laughed, in Japanese we laughed together.

Then I went out on the porch and opened my Obento. Everything was so delicious. It was the first time that I really enjoyed it—all the good things that mother had packed for me.

Bus

I started Loomis Union Grammar School in September of 1928. The school was in town about four miles from where we lived so I rode the school bus. Waiting for the bus with my books and lunch pail in the morning, I was afraid it would roar past me but remarkably the driver saw me waiting and always stopped. I couldn't believe it.

Though intimidated by the older and louder children on the bus, I was glad to get on. I remember how stuffy it was inside the bus, especially on rainy days when the icing glass windows were closed. The bus smelled of heavy clothing and warm bodies and garlic sausage sandwiches in some of the bag lunches. Mercifully, it was a short ride to school.

Buses made several trips and I was assigned the second run going home after school. That gave me time to play—a dangerous temptation I was soon to discover. Once I became so involved in a game of bomb with a friend that I completely forgot about my bus. When I remembered, the bus had come and gone. That lost feeling I experienced at that moment has haunted me ever since. Fortunately, an older boy who had worked at our place the previous summer found me crying. He brought me to Mr. Bates, the principal of the school. I had never met Mr. Bates but I knew he was someone to fear. Teachers were always threatening to send us to Mr. Bates if we misbehaved. I didn't know what to make of him. But Mr. Bates turned out to be a gentle, kindly man, who assured me everything would be all right, and he drove me home with the older boy showing the way.

My parents could not believe that the principal of the school had driven four miles out to the country to bring me home. "Are you telling the truth?" they asked again and again and I kept saying, "Yes, yes, Mr. Bates brought me home."

They were pleased and grateful, even honored; in appreciation, they surprised Mr. Bates with a present at Christmas.

1928

1928 was a good year for my father. I believe he made some money, even if the gross income had to be considerable; he had to share it with the owner on a 50/50 basis and his share would be what was left after the monthly living advances were deducted. Still, I think he made enough to consider making a change in his life.

It was also the year mother had a problem. After the fruitful summer, her allergies became so bad that she had to see a doctor, who told her that she was suffering from hay fever. There was no cure except to avoid the pollens from the grasses, weeds, and trees. The way she suffered—nonstop sneezing, watery, itchy eyes, runny nose—it was a serious concern for my parents. Of course, it precluded her living and working on the farm.

What a blow this was, right after their most financially rewarding year. What could they do? Farming was their lifeblood. After much discussion that extended over several days and nights, it was decided that mother and we three children would go to Japan. We had only heard of Japan from our parents but we were going on a trip, a long boat trip that we had never taken before. We looked forward to this new adventure.

I don't know whose idea it was; probably father's, since mother in her situation didn't have much say. After eight and a half

KASHIWAGI FAMILY PORTRAIT. LEFT TO RIGHT, FOLLOWED BY AGE: HIROSHI (6), FUKUMATSU (FATHER, 39), KOFUSA (MOTHER, 25), EIKO (SISTER, 3), RYO (BROTHER, 4 1/2). (LOOMIS, CALIFORNIA, CA. AUG.1928).

years in America, I think she rather welcomed the chance to rejoin her family in Japan. Though drastic, it was in keeping with father's plan of making enough money so he could return to Japan with his family. Only now he was sending us ahead as he, himself, would remain in America to make the rest of his fortune to realize his dream.

So in preparation for our trip, we went to Sacramento, where father's photographer friend took our family photograph and the individual passport pictures. Though considerably retouched, the group photo shows father looking manly and handsome and mother youthful and attractive with her hair done in waves which was the style at the time; she had been to a beauty shop. We kids are standing in front in stepladder row, looking stiff and awkward in our new outfits. I was six and a half, my brother five and sister four. It's a good portrait of the family, actually: my favorite.

Before our passports came through, however, father learned that the fish market/grocery store in town was up for sale. The owners, having made enough money after five years, were selling out and returning to Japan. This news called for another meeting. Mother was twenty-six and father at forty was in his prime. They really didn't want to be separated. Father, who had been a fisherman in San Pedro, certainly knew about fish. In fact, he had some friends who were fish dealers in San Pedro from where the fresh fish would be shipped via railway express. As for running a business, my father had operated a small cafe in Los Angeles and later a diner on Second Street in Sacramento, catering to workingmen and bums. Though only a small enterprise, the fish market was definitely a move upward. For mother, too, it was a new experience. She would be living in town, away from the farm and best of all, she would not suffer from hay fever. Father dropped his earlier plan and bought the store.

So I became a "townie," beginning with my second year at Loomis Union Grammar School, walking the short distance to school, even coming home for lunch, making some new non-Japanese friends along the way.

I realize now what a turning point this was in my life. I could have been a victim of the nationalistic fervor that was sweeping Japan at the time. I often wonder how I would have fared there. I was young enough that I would have adjusted to life in Japan, though with some difficulty. After a year of grammar school, I was beginning to understand English, even feel faint stirrings of being American. I would have been different enough in Japan to be regarded an outsider and probably the object of taunts from the native kids. Living with relatives would have been difficult, even though father would have sent money for our keep as he had promised. Would I have been caught up in the rise of militarism, the fanatic nationalism and the Emperor worship that pervaded Japan in the thirties? I know I would have hated the compulsory military training in the school. I wonder how I would have reacted to the propaganda and the brainwashing which were parts of Japan at that time. As a child of adventurous emigrants who had left Japan and as an outsider, I would have been confused and probably miserable. At any rate, I am grateful for my parents' decision to remain in America where I would grow up as a Nisei or an American-born citizen of Japanese parents. Of course, I did not anticipate the problems I would encounter as a Japanese American.

Pee in the Puddle

Wes was fat something
of a classroom joke
we laughed when he
was late which was
almost everyday and
we laughed when he
came on time John
was always so fair
he let me play
Chinese tag with
them on the way
home from school
but I like to remember
him as our fourth
grade Santa Claus
though actually he
was slender with
a high nose and
very German it was
he who thought we

should pee in the
puddle he called
our things brownies
I know he got it
from mine theirs
were white blue
white I wonder
what became of
Wes I know John
was killed during
World War II
flying for the RAF
crazy guy couldn't
wait for the US
to enter the war
I suppose Wes is
still fat and lazy
probably a father many times

anyway we wasted
a lot of time
after school three
golden loops rising
out of the
brown puddle into
which in time we
all three were
shoved when at
last I came home
crying for my
bread and jam I
was smelling quite
a bit of pee
remembering now
I can almost
smell it Wes's
John's and mine.

Boyhood in Loomis

I spent most of my boyhood in Loomis until my father quit the store in 1940. Then we moved to Penryn, three miles east, where we lived until we were ordered out by President Roosevelt's Executive Order 9066.

Loomis is about 20 miles northeast of Sacramento. When I was growing up Highway 40, or the Lincoln Highway, ran through the town in front of our store. I would spend long hours sitting out on the front porch and watch the cars drive past. Ostensibly, I was watching the store but until a customer came, this is what I did: I would let my imagination run wild and hitch a ride on a car going east to Lake Tahoe or Reno, or a car going west to Sacramento or even San Francisco. Our dog Prince, who had a thing about cars, would break my reverie by barking and chasing after the front wheel of the cars. Sometimes I would recognize the same car I had seen going in the morning, returning in the late afternoon or evening, probably after a day of revelry at the lake or in the snow, depending on the time of the year.

The fruit house—Pacific Fruit Exchange—right across the highway, was another source of diversion, especially during the fruit season in the summer. The farmers would back their trucks, loaded with crates of fruit, to the loading dock and the crates would be trucked into the fruit shed. Later, they would be loaded into the refrigerated car and transported to Chicago, New York, Boston and other markets in the east. The fruits from Placer County—plums, peaches, and pears—were much sought after in the markets and brought good prices. I remember my father talking with the farmers about the F.O.B. (free on board) prices and the returns on the account sales, only they would call them "conseru."

Beyond the fruit shed were the train tracks where the interminable freight trains rumbled by every day at the scheduled times. But it was at night when I heard the train whistle in the distance that I experienced the strange, lonely feeling of being in touch with the mysteries of the universe, like a glance at the night sky, full of stars, being moved, not knowing why.

We used to make and sell tofu. I say "we" because, though I was seven or eight years old, I was very much involved with making tofu. Although father had been a fisherman, he knew nothing about making tofu; he had to learn from the folks who had the store before him. The only problem was the tofu they made was notoriously bad. People joked and said you could toss the tofu like a ball and it wouldn't fall apart. There were constant complaints from the customers: "Kashiwagi-san, why can't you make better tofu?" to which father turned a deaf ear. But when they stopped buying the tofu and father had to throw out more than he sold, then he realized he better do something about it.

So he went to the tofu house in Sacramento ostensibly to buy tofu but his main purpose was to see how they made it. After several such "buying" trips and some experimentation at home, he had mastered the secret of making good tofu that had something to do with how he stirred the nigari (bittern) that separated the curds and the whey. At any rate, he was able to make excellent tofu, a clone of the Sacramento tofu, one might say. People praised the new tofu lavishly and we could hardly keep up with the demand. Even today when I eat tofu made in Sacramento, I can taste our tofu.

Recently, I told this story at a community program in San

Francisco and before I could sit down, a man in the back got up and said, "I'm the son of that Sacramento tofu maker. I wonder if there's a lawyer in the house."

He stopped me for a moment but luckily he was only joking; his comment and my momentary befuddlement brought down the house. I guess that was his reward.

What was difficult about my tofu-making chore was that I could not leave the one-horse power motor slowly moving the stone grinder, not even to relieve myself, until the work was done, a stretch of over two hours. I had to make sure that the water was dripping properly and the grinder was always filled with bloated beans. If it ran on empty there would be dire consequences—the grinder would run amok, the motor would start to smoke, etc. Fearful of this happening, I stuck to my job.

But I like tofu—always did, and I'm glad it has become a part of the American diet.

Tofu

tofu
white blocks
of bean cake
good
protein food
I know
sure I know
two hours
every day
after school
I spent
grinding soy beans
into a
frothy mess
washtubful
for papa's
famous
fine-textured
number one

three for a
quarter
tofu
good
for you
not for me
too much
of my
boyhood
went into
good
protein food
now white folks
now vegetarians
have discovered
tofu
they eat it
praise it
even make it
tofu
good
for you
not for me
the goddamned
tofu

Hard Times

I t was the time of the Great Depression in the early thirties when it was hard times for everyone. There were no jobs to be had and no food, but those who lived in the country were fortunate: they could grow their own vegetables and raise chickens, rabbits, pigs, even goats for milk. Since it was a fruit-growing district, fruits of all kinds were plentiful in season and the surplus was preserved for winter.

We were lucky that father ran a store; I don't remember ever going hungry. We lived in the back and we could raid the store for food. We even had candy. We weren't allowed to have big bars that cost five cents, but we had any number of penny suckers, licorice, Butterfingers, and plenty of little caramels that came four or five to a penny— not that we ever paid. It's a wonder we still have teeth, for all the cheap candy we ate.

Mother always had things ready for the steady stream of men who came to the back door for handouts. These men, mostly white, with hat in hand, were grateful for anything that mother had for them—bread ends, crackers, leftovers, even rice. Though threadbare and grimy, their clothes were well cut. The tramps were part of the daily scene but sometimes mother complained. "Urusai na,"(how bothersome), she said when her work in the kitchen was interrupted. But she never disappointed them.

"I'm busier at the back door than in the front," she joked. Meanwhile, father was falling deeper and deeper into debt. The wholesalers who were providing the mostly imported staples of course wanted their payment, and father was hard put to find ways to pay them or keep them satisfied enough that they would continue to supply him. Poor father was caught in the middle; he had to extend credit to the farmers who were always behind in their payments. Once he went to a family whose bill was way past due and when he asked for payment, the man pointed to the outhouse and said, "It's all there; get it from there."

Father didn't deserve to take such abuse. But the farmers just couldn't pay; they were living on about thirty-five dollars a month, if that much, in advance on the crop which might or might not pay off after the harvest; meanwhile, the whole family worked the farm the year round. Sometimes they would bring vegetables or live chickens in gunny sacks in exchange for shoyu (soy sauce), rice, miso (bean paste), sugar, tea, and other staples. This was fine for us, but it didn't help our creditors.

I remember one night, a rainy night around nine o'clock, father had us all in the bedroom. Suddenly, we heard someone calling and father said, "Turn off the lights!" So there we were, huddled in the dark—father, mother, brother, sister and I—pretending not to be there; we kids didn't know what to make of the situation; was it a game? Yet adults were playing it. Outside in the rain, we heard the salesman calling, "Kashiwagi-san, Kashiwagi-san!" He must have known that we were inside. The rain seemed especially loud.

After a moment, I heard mother say, "Shouldn't we let him in?" "Quiet," father whispered, "besides, it's too late now; what would we tell him?"

The man continued to call while we remained very still. Finally, he gave up and went away. I guess it was a mean trick to play on him (he had to make a living too), but I don't think father liked him much. He said the young salesman was a smartass from San Francisco; father didn't do that to his other creditors.

We somehow managed to survive the Depression, though it was hard on father. Maybe that's why he developed TB so early in his life.

I once wrote a play about our store, titling it *Live Oak Store.* Actually, our store was called Loomis Fish Market, but this was a play, and "Live Oak" somehow better conveyed the idea of survival that was the main theme of the play.

There was a live oak tree behind the billboard where I had a bird's eye view of the town. Across Lincoln Highway, which ran in front was the fruit house and beyond, was the railroad track where long freight trains came on schedule and an occasional passenger train. Sitting up there, I felt I had access to the whole world, the trains bringing the world to me. Sometimes, I would board one of the trains for an imaginary trip. I had been as far as Sacramento, so things were familiar up to that point, but beyond that was pure fantasy and I let my imagination run wild.

It was also a time when many folks were hitchhiking just as in the old Clark Gable movie *It Happened One Night*, though I didn't see this movie until years later. If I managed to stay hidden in the oak tree and remained very quiet, not even breathing, I could spy on people who came behind the billboard to relieve themselves.

Live Oak Store

sitting atop the billboard
that said
"I'd walk a mile for a Camel"
I saw
a man and woman
peeing
then standing up
they began
to fuck
it was the depression
there were no beds
and such
not even food
only love
on the run
watched by a
bug-eyed kid
who got so tense
he nearly
fell through
the live oak branch
to join
the festivity

Mr. Swift

Mr. Swift was not a big person, as Americans go, but he was an important man in town. He was the proprietor of Swift's Grocery and lived on a ranch that he owned in the country. We didn't know much about his ranch, as no Japanese had ever worked or lived there.

"Hello sonny."

"Hello."

"I'm Mr. Swift," he said and instantly I was struck by the fact that he had addressed himself as "Mr. Swift." We Japanese don't do that and even I, an eight-year-old, was aware of that. We would say, "I am Swift." I wondered why he addressed himself as "Mr. Swift." Was he that important? Was it because he was a hakujin, a white American? They often did strange things.

"I'd like to talk to your daddy, is he in?"

"No, Mr. Swift."

"When will he be back?" He asked gently enough, yet I was a little frightened since his nose was pointed at me. I turned to mother, who was staring at some papers in Mr. Swift's hand. I interpreted the question.

"Tell Mr. Swift, papa will be back at supper time," mother said, still looking at the papers. I told Mr. Swift and he smiled pleasantly and we all smiled.

FUKUMATSU KASHIWAGI. (LOOMIS, CALIFORNIA, CA.1931)

"I'll be back later," Mr. Swift said, leaving.

It had ended so quickly that I was a little sorry, but mother looked worried.

"What were those papers?" She wondered aloud.

"He didn't say, mama."

"I know he didn't. That's what worries me," mother said. She was always afraid of papers in English and it was because of father.

"Don't ever take up pen or brush, no matter what they say," he always told her. "Just remember you don't know English and don't pretend to understand," he warned her repeatedly. This was funny because I often caught father laughing and nodding with hakujin even when I knew he didn't understand what they were saying. He just knew that Americans joked a lot and were pleased when you laughed at their jokes, whether you understood them or not.

Father came home soon and we told him about Mr. Swift and his papers.

"What kind of papers?"

"I don't know," I said, before I realized father hated this answer. This made him very impatient with me, but I always forgot.

"Why didn't you ask him?"

"He wanted to see you, papa, and he was here only a minute," mother said, speaking for me. I didn't say anything after that, and we ate supper in silence.

Then we heard Mr. Swift come in, and father went out to meet him. I followed, as I was needed to interpret for them.

"I believe you're Mr. ..."

"Kashiwagi."

"Yes, Well, I'm Mr. Swift," he said, extending his hand which father took. There it was again, referring to himself as "Mr. Swift," when would he ever learn? He continued, "I was here a while ago, but you weren't in. Have you had dinner?" There was a pause and I interpreted.

"Ask Mr. Swift what he wants," father said.

"My father would like to know what you want."

"Oh, of course," Mr. Swift said, bringing out the papers again. "I have here an agreement signed by all the merchants in town. We're all working together and I thought your father would like to join us."

This was quite long and difficult and I had trouble explaining. "But what does he want?" father said, his voice and face showing impatience. He turned directly to Mr. Swift and asked, "What you want?" I could tell Mr. Swift was a bit taken aback.

"All right, I'll come to the point. We want you to sign this agreement not to do business on Sundays." Father turned to me and I explained what he had already guessed.

"No sign," father said.

"But Mr. Kashi...."

"Kashiwagi."

"Yes, you must cooperate with us."

"No," father said again. I guess he wanted to explain that his store was mainly for Japanese customers, that few Japanese shopped at the other stores. That in fact, they wouldn't be served there and no Japanese would risk that humiliation; that the Japanese were working farmers whose only time off was on an occasional Sunday when they could come to shop; that he had hardly any non-Japanese customers even on Sundays; that there was no law forbidding Sunday openings; that it was all absurd and there was no need to talk any further. But father's English was inadequate, and he was beyond patience with me.

"Does your father understand what I'm saying?"

"I no understand close Sunday," father said before I could interpret the question.

"Why you must understand, this is a Christian town, and there should not be any business transactions of any kind on the Sabbath." I thought father snorted at this.

"You better sign this," Mr. Swift said, slamming down the papers on the counter.

Father looked straight at Mr. Swift. "Tell Mr. Swift to go," he said, walking away.

"Your father doesn't seem to understand. This," Mr. Swift said, shaking the papers, "is for the good of the town. I hope your father believes in goodwill. Will you explain that to him?"

"Yes."

"And tell him, we haven't seen the end of this," Mr. Swift said as he left, the screen door banging loudly after him. I was glad it was over. This was an adult problem, a fearful one, with all the tensions underlying it, and I felt caught in the middle.

Haircut

Papa
you used to
cut my hair
rice bowl style
carving
big ears for
juicy spitball
targets
Papa
you used to
work your mouth
in time to the
hand clipper
you were a
happy craftsman
as long as I sat
perfectly still
but if I so much as
winced
when you

pulled my hair
you were offended
you became
impatient
you lost your craft
you pulled more hair
I suffered
the haircut
suffered
when I cried
ouch
you even
bopped me
on the head

one bright
Sunday morning
a shadow crossed
the light
a tall hakujin
grinned down at us
hello there
mind if I
take a picture
for the
Sacramento Bee

Jap hating
yellow paper
Papa
you snatched the
newspaper
pinned around me
scattering hair
in several
directions
get hell out
you roared
the tall hakujin
fled
the camera
on a strap
bouncing
on his back
you were
agitated
of course
but Papa
that was the
worst haircut
you ever gave me
for two weeks

I had to wear
a stocking cap
in and out
of the
classroom
but Papa
it's the haircut
I remember most
it's the haircut
I most associate
with you

FAMILY PICNIC. "CAP BOYS." LEFT TO RIGHT: HIROSHI KASHIWAGI (8), MIKIO KONDA (NOW DECEASED, 6-7), RYO KASHIWAGI (6-7), AND FUMIO KUBO (6-7). (LOOMIS, CALIFORNIA, MARCH 8, 1931)

Prince

My first live dog was Prince, who came as part of the store. Prince, part bulldog, was a first-class watchdog, ferocious and menacing to strangers, not letting a soul set foot in our backyard, but gentle with family members and friends. An outside dog, he was hardly a pet.

He had a chronic skin ailment and was constantly scratching himself, usually on the edge of father's truck fender. I remember hosing him from a distance; that was his bath. He would bark and jump at the stream of water. I suppose he enjoyed it. Sometimes I aimed the stream at his scrotum and Prince played along with me like a patient, understanding adult tolerating the silly antics of a kid. He was devoted to father. Every afternoon he would sit by the gate and wait for father's return. Father always looked for him, too. They were great companions, a familiar sight in town, walking to and from the post office or the bank.

Prince's one weakness was chasing cars and barking at the wheel, a futile endeavor but one that seemed to obsess him. It proved fatal some years later in 1937 when he was found dead on the street, having been hit by a car, no doubt the one he was chasing. But by then he was old and spiritless, perhaps carrying some of the burden of the unhappiness in our family at that time.

But Prince was the cause—at least the immediate cause that we could tell—of the most terrifying night of my childhood.

One evening, we were all sitting in the kitchen, which was also our parlor. We heard Prince bark; it was a savage alarming bark, a kind we had never heard before. Presently, we heard a rough voice and a sharp cry from the dog, then heavy footsteps on our back porch, followed by a rap that was at once threatening. Father opened the door and there stood a huge white American. His bare arms were hairy and immense, and his angry face was flushed. Father stepped outside wondering if the man had been bothered by Prince.

"Come 'ere," the stranger said, "how many more like you."

We were huddled by the door, too terrified to move, as the stranger glared at each of us and counted us off with a long finger. "Goodbye, five Japs," he threatened. Father stepped off the porch and told mother to look after us.

The two were now sparring in the yard where we played our games, but this was no make-believe game. This was so real, we couldn't believe it was happening. Father looked like a child next to the huge white American, who kept swinging wildly as father dodged and weaved. Then with all the strength of his body, father struck his fist against the stranger's jaw. It was a powerful blow. The man's face was cut but it only seemed to shake him out of his stupor. He was really mad now.

Unable to think, mother and we children ran around crying and screaming, "Papa, Papa." Then suddenly mother stopped. "Saloon," she shouted and grabbed my arm and we both raced to the back door of the saloon. Mother had never approved of our neighbor; even now, she held on to me and wouldn't let me go in, but we yelled and screamed. Mother's poor English, which was always something of a joke, now burst forth, loud and compelling, "Man fight! Com' help! Hurry up, hurry up!"

After a moment the saloon owner came out and we rushed him to the fight scene.

The American kept swinging wildly and each time he missed

his fury mounted. Father could only dodge and protect himself. Cautiously, he retreated. He noticed a shovel leaning against the house and moved toward it. Now he grabbed it and held it up like a Japanese sword, daring the giant to rush for the blade end. The man lunged and father pulled and the giant, all six feet of him, hurtled to the ground at father's feet. Father pounced on him and locked his arm around the man's neck. The American struggled violently as father slowly tightened the chokehold; the man grabbed father's thumb and tried to bend it and father savagely sank his teeth into the back of the hairy hand. The man let go of the thumb. The blood seemed to drain from his face and his struggles stopped. Still father didn't relax his hold. Finally the man tapped father's thigh, once, twice, and again weakly.

"Let him go," the saloon owner said.

"You take him away?" Father asked.

"Yeah."

We hurried into the house and father bolted the door.

"It was lucky you got the saloon owner. I was going to drop him," father said

"Are you hurt? Are you hurt?" mother asked. "Oh," she said when she spotted some blood on his face. Wiping it off with a towel, she discovered it was the American's blood.

"What a scare," she said.

"Everything is all right now," father said and told us children to go to bed.

As I lay in bed, I kept going over the fight. What if father had taken one of those powerful blows? What if he had been knocked out? Surely, the stranger would have come after us. And what if father had dropped him? I imagined that that meant to kill him. What a frightening thought. How fortunate that we were still alive, that we had survived this terrible night, that the stranger was too still alive. Why was he so angry? Was it because of Prince? But what was he doing in our backyard? These troubling questions kept me from falling asleep. For a long time I heard the murmur of my parents in the kitchen. I was proud of my brave father. Then I heard my mother laugh; father must have said something to break the tension. I was thankful that we were still a family, bonded as never before by the mad and frightful happening of the night. My brother and sister were already asleep. After a while I too fell asleep.

The next day when father went to the post office, he was hailed, ironically, a town hero. The folks marveled at how this small man had subdued the giant intruder. "Lucky," was all father said. Lucky indeed. It was a matter of survival, life or death for him and possibly for his family. A danger dogged him every day, one that only an outsider like father would know and understand.

At Omoto's

As it turned out, Prince was the first to know. He was barking at the men who were planting the stakes for the new highway which would come through the middle of our house. The markers confirmed the rumors that the store would be torn down, making way for the project of President Roosevelt's New Deal program.

I am sure it didn't take much to bring down the old wooden structure, probably the oldest in Loomis. One day after school I went back to look and it was gone—a big emptiness where the store had been. It was difficult to imagine that we had lived there until a few days before. And where had all the rats gone? We had shared the place with them, large fearless creatures that came out, day or night, to forage, often ignoring our presence. I imagined they too were forced to seek another place to live.

Just as we got the order to move, father came down with pleurisy and was hospitalized in Sacramento. Baby Fusako was four months old. Mother faced the daunting task of closing the store and moving out the stocks and fixtures as well as the furniture and the household effects. Friends came forward with their trucks and their open hearts, assuring mother that everything would be all right, not to worry. I was a kid and didn't fully realize how the friends rescued us from the misfortune that had befallen us. Though it is too late to thank them as most have passed on, I want to acknowledge here the many acts of kindness and compassion that we received from our friends at a time when we were most desperate. The most generous was Mr. Omoto who offered us a place to live.

The cabin where we stayed had three rooms: a bedroom on each end and a room in the middle that served as a kitchen where mother cooked and where we took our meals and did our homework. In the summer, when it was unbearably hot, we spent as little time as we could in the house. My brother and I shared a room that was also a storeroom, piled high with trunks and boxes that barely left enough space for our bed and dresser. In the other room there were two beds, one for my parents and the other for my sister and the baby. A table separated the beds.

It was crowded but cozy, especially in the winter when the wood stove warmed the entire cabin. In the evenings, we sat around the stove, huddled together, our features softened by the orange glow of the kerosene lamp, casting large shadows in the room. The shadows were comforting, like other presences in the room.

Father often suggested that we make pancakes at night and mother's usual comment was "Isn't it late?" She was teasing us but we always fell for it. Soon she was gathering the ingredients and mixing milk, flour, baking powder, sugar, and salt and pouring the batter into the frying pan, filling it completely. It was our "dango," or one huge pancake that we broke up and shared among us, eating it with butter and homemade blackberry jam. Water from the well was stored in a barrel that stood just outside the door.

We were quite happy living there. Everyone in the family made us feel at home, carrying out the authority of Mr. Omoto. The six children shared everything with the three of us who were always around, including us in all their activities. Despite this, I could never, not even for a moment, forget that I was an outsider, dependent on their kindness, generosity, and even charity.

I think I was like Prince who was chained to his doghouse.

Though the chain was quite long, giving him considerable latitude, it was still a restraint on his freedom. I remember how happy he had been when we first moved there, running around the yard, exploring strange new sights and smells. But when he became too rambunctious, chasing cats, other dogs, and chickens, father decided to keep Prince chained. How listless and unhappy he looked whenever I took him his food. He was not a dog to pet, but I remember wanting to do so. It was cruel to keep him chained.

I myself wasn't exactly chained, but neither was I a normal carefree child, always wary of saying or doing something that might annoy or upset the Omotos. I was overly sensitive, guarded like an adult, hence not always happy.

Once when we were playing on the floor—I don't remember what it was, some card game or jacks—anyway, we were on our knees, crowded together, and my sister, wanting to make room for herself, said, "Get out," to one of the boys. She meant to say, "Move over; give me some space," but his retort was: "You get out, this is not your place!"

That was like a slap across my face. I could not react to him; I dared not; instead, I wanted to scream at my sister for being so dumb, for making herself so vulnerable but I kept quiet. After a mild admonishment by one of the older siblings, they all resumed playing. I wanted to leave, pulling my sister after me but where would we go? Where could we go? I sat quietly, desperately practicing bushido, a form of stoicism that I had learned in kendo (Japanese fencing).

Father was recuperating from his bout with pleurisy but he was not one to sit idly, especially when he felt deeply obligated to Mr. Omoto and his family. He began to work the farm, at first tentatively, a few hours a day, pruning trees. However, before long he was putting in full days, despite mother's warning to be careful. Of course, he never listened to her. He felt fine, why shouldn't he work at full capacity. After pruning was over, it was time for plowing. Father loved horses and was an expert at plowing.

Plowing is hard work, guiding the horse and plow, being pulled all day, walking endless miles over uneven footing. It is daunting even for someone in good physical health. When father slept at night, exhausted from a full day of plowing, mother noticed a strange sound in his breathing. This, they later realized, was the onset of the tuberculosis that would plague father the rest of his life. Mother pleaded with him to see a doctor but he refused, continuing to work. Meanwhile, the TB bacteria were eating away at his lungs. In time he began to lose weight and developed a cough.

I was eleven when I learned to pick fruits using an eight-foot ladder. I must have been well trained because by the time I was fourteen, I was a regular fruit picker working ten hours a day, earning close to adult wages. I was a left-handed picker. (I guess I am ambidextrous; whenever I favor my right side, I feel a longing ache in my left hand and arm, which probably were often neglected.) I also made boxes or crates for plums and peaches. I had done this from the time I was five but now at eleven and twelve I was a bit more adept and faster. I believe I was paid fifty cents a day. At the end of harvest, I remember Mr. Omoto calling me to his desk and handing me a check. A wonderful man, Mr. Omoto made this a ceremony that I would never forget. To me the check was a princely sum that I promptly gave to father. I don't know what he did with it, probably bought school clothes for me.

After two years father felt ready to go back on his own. Encouraged by Mr. Omoto, who loaned him some startup money, he found a vacant building in town that he could fix up for his fish market/grocery store.

It was the summer before my eighth and final year at Loomis Union Grammar School when I went along to assist him to build the counters, the display tables, and make the back area habitable for the family. Sometimes I helped by holding the board steady when he sawed or nailed, but mainly I was there as his companion. The work took about two weeks. I remember it fondly as a time when I was closest to my father. This man who could be so fierce and violent was gentle and loving with me, so pleased that I was there with him. He called me "Hiro-chan," the loving diminutive, like I was still a little boy. It could have been the happiest time of his life—those two weeks. I was happy too as we were preparing to be independent, have our own place, free again. I didn't realize how much I had missed being free until the day we moved in when, unlike my usual guarded self, I kept grinning and running around, not caring about what people thought of me. I was back to being myself—a carefree 13-year-old.

Plowing

my father
was good with horses
he smelled like one
molded to the plow
just a touch
of the reins
and the horse
responded
skipping over
the straight
straight furrow
I turn around
and find blackbirds
frolicking
on the
new-turned earth

American River

Swimming was our principal recreation in the summer. We could not go unless the temperature hit 90 degrees or above—so we put the thermometer out in the sun, sometimes shaking it impatiently, and barely waited until it reached 90. Then we rushed off with our swimming trunks to our favorite swimming hole in the American River, about four miles away. How exciting it was going, standing in the back of the pickup truck. I learned to swim the summer I was eleven and in the process nearly drowned.

After three Sundays of practice, I thought I was ready to cross the river, a distance of about ten yards, doing the crawl stroke; others were doing the dog paddle. I had learned the stroke from an older boy who was visiting from Sacramento; he called it the "Australian crawl," a rather showy style with elaborate arm movements. Of course, I hadn't learned to breathe properly so I held my breath as I made the plunge. I was doing fine for five or six strokes, then, for some reason, I stopped; maybe I needed air or thought I had made the crossing. I hadn't. I was vertical, my eyes were full of water. I couldn't touch bottom. I panicked and cried for help. The older boy named Hal, who was watching me, tossed an inflated tire tube but I was blinded and couldn't see so he dived in and pulled me to shore. It was a scare that I never forgot.

It was my first real challenge in life and my first failure; I felt foolish, but mercifully no one faulted me for trying. Recently, I related the incident to Hal's widow who was completely unaware of it and she and I shared a moment, remembering Hal, appreciating the kind selfless person he was.

Father, who was downstream and had observed it all, said later, "I was waiting to pull you out when you came downstream." I couldn't understand his remark; I thought it was callous considering I had nearly drowned. But father was a strong, confident swimmer; his dives from a high boulder were spectacular. Mother, too, was a fair swimmer, with her rather busy sidestrokes. She had grown up near a river where she and her brother used to swim in the summer.

In 1989, six years after Mother's death, my wife and I visited my uncle and aunt in Wakayama. Uncle hired a taxi and we drove about an hour to the old homesite. Mother always said she came from deep in the "inaka" (country). It was rural all right, but beautiful. I wish I could have convinced mother of that. To the north was a forest of trees, and to the west on a hill was where my grandfather had worked his crops. The land had been sold after grandmother's death, and the house was gone, but down to the south was the river where uncle and mother had played in the summers. "I can still picture us swimming in the river," uncle said, recalling the happy days of their childhood.

Soon after our return from camp, we were again swimming in the American River. It was a hot day and we were there primarily to cool off. My brother and I were the only ones who could swim. Others were using pillowcases that they inflated and held as floats, a dangerous device we soon discovered when a pillowcase used by a teenage girl deflated. She screamed for help. I went in after her and she grabbed me and we both started to go down. It was quite deep and while we descended I remember saying to myself, "Here we go." I was completely relaxed and I remember a strange feeling of exhilaration; it seemed like we were entering a totally new realm, like Urashimataro, the fisherman in the

Japanese folk tale. We were in a watery kingdom inhabited by beautiful mermaids. We soon hit bottom and bounded up and somehow I managed to get my companion to shore. It was rather messy, especially after the miracle of the previous moment. When the girl later thanked me for saving her life, I was embarrassed; I didn't feel heroic at all.

Chocolate Cake

*H*is name was Thomas Paine. He was bigger and older than most of us. He was often seen driving his family touring car with the top down and a tiny birdlike woman (his mother we assumed) seated in the back. We were in the eighth grade and most of us knew how to drive but we didn't dare venture out in public, on the highway or on the busy county roads. We didn't have a license, so we drove only at the ranch or on the back roads. How could Thomas Paine be driving through town? Did he really have a license to drive? How old was he?

He was absent from class a lot. I don't know what he gave as his excuse, but he couldn't have been sick all those times. He was probably running errands with his mother. I don't think he ever studied; whenever he was called on by the teacher he had a ready answer, a wild guess. Sometimes he was right, but more often he wasn't. When he was wrong he would grin or even laugh and the teacher, who wasn't put off by this, reprimanded him for not doing his homework. He was often late for class but we knew when he was coming by the noise his hightop boots made in the hallway.

"Thomas Paine," we said in anticipation.

We always called him Thomas Paine. I suppose because we knew that that was a famous name, though they were not related.

He was a class distraction. We were aware of him when he was present and also when he wasn't. But none of us was close to him—not that this concerned him very much.

He had a wooly feel about him, always bundled up in heavy clothing—sweater, coat, muffler, cap. His clothes fit him loosely which made him look bigger than he actually was. He didn't seem to bathe too often. We Japanese were especially conscious of this, as we ourselves bathed every night. His thick, dark hair was usually uncombed.

One day a class party was planned. There had to be some excuse for it but I can't remember what it was. What I do remember was the chocolate cake that Thomas Paine brought to the party. We had asked him to bring something and he had readily agreed, which was a surprise. What was he bringing? He didn't say; he kept us guessing; always the mysterious Thomas Paine. Still, we were afraid he might be absent on the day of the party. It was very possible.

He was late. So we went ahead with the party and then he appeared, carrying a metal cake box that had a rather ornate handle on top and two clamps on the bottom. Inside, was a beautiful three-layered cake, large enough for the whole class—fine-textured, dark cake covered with the smoothest chocolate icing that melted in the mouth. Of course, it was homemade. The best cake we ever tasted, we all exclaimed, wishing for another piece. For days afterward we talked about Thomas Paine's chocolate cake; in fact, he was on our minds more than ever and our esteem for him rose to such a height that we would have voted him head monitor, king of the class, best friend, whatever he pleased. And Thomas Paine seemed to enjoy his newfound popularity; he came to school every day.

Then it was May and all our thoughts were directed toward our impending graduation—the final tests to study for and pass; the traditional picnic outing with the seventh grade class; the proper clothing for the graduation (the girls in white dresses and the boys in white shirts, blue ties, and dark wool trousers, in

June?!); the class picture and the ceremony itself—we would march in to "Finlandia," gamely played by the school orchestra, the class would sing "School Days," Mr. Bates, our principal, would speak to us, and the school board president would hand out our diplomas. I guess Thomas Paine wasn't involved in much of these activities; he seemed to have reverted to his old ways— always tardy, frequently absent, sometimes for several days in a row—and then he was gone altogether. He either quit school or moved away. He is conspicuously absent from the class picture.

I wish he had graduated with us. But who can forget him, Thomas Paine, the classmate with the illustrious name, the boy who one day brought that marvelous gift to the class—the luscious chocolate cake that will remain forever in our memory as the best we ever tasted in our whole life. Even after all these years, none has ever come close to Thomas Paine's cake, the cake his mother made for us.

Dominguez

I was thinking of Dominguez Mendoza, wondering if he was still alive. I owe him a treat, a milkshake treat. It sounds silly but it happened when I was fourteen.

I couldn't tell Dominguez or anybody from the twenty or more Filipino men out in the ranch. They all seemed alike to me—the same dark faces, the bandana neckerchiefs, the light quick feet, and the Tagalog speech. I kept away from them as much as I could, though we were doing the same thing, picking Santa Rosa plums. We even drank water from the same canteen, though none of the men drank half as much as I did. I guess I was afraid of them. I had heard stories about how handy they were with knives and how they thought nothing of sticking one in a man's heart. It didn't sound too chummy, the way they talked back and forth, and any minute I expected them to start slinging daggers or one of those trick knives people said they carried. Nothing like that ever happened but I was always looking for it.

Father always said, "You can't trust those Filipinos," and I believed him, for he had his troubles with them. He liked to get their trade selling them groceries, but the real challenge was getting paid. They practically bought out the store—a crate of assorted vegetables, piles of canned goods and pounds of fish. And I can't say father didn't slip them a tired fish now and then.

He did, but that was after he found he couldn't trust them. Everything was on credit and about five of the men, leaders I supposed or proud ones, who could write, each signed his name to the bill. Beautiful handwriting too, and names like music— Richard Bello, Carlos Esteban, Dominguez Mendoza—but darn if father could remember them for a minute.

One summer the men forgot to pay and father chased them all the way to Sacramento. But they got away easily, scattering to pool halls, hotels, bars, and other likely places. They could have stood around on the sidewalk with their hands in their pockets, for there were hundreds of them, all in neat fancy outfits and father could never tell who was who. He lost nearly $60, which was quite a sum for a small store in those days. He got wise to them by asking the boss to give him early notice of payday so he could be around for his share. I guess he didn't have much trouble after that; anyway, I didn't see him suddenly chasing off to Sacramento.

I was 14 and I could pick plums. I had picked them since I was 10 years old. Of course, every new season I had to learn all over again, but after a couple of days I could size the plums at a glance. I could tell which was packed 5x5's, 4x5's, and 4x4's. I knew the colors too. I knew what was half-color, quarter-color, straw-color, and green-color. I could also handle the 8-foot ladder better than anyone else. It was heavy but I didn't move it around much—just poked it in between the branches, four or five places, and I had circled the tree and was moving on to the next.

"Always stay one tree ahead of the others," father said. He was interested in my work; he didn't want me fired. I did what he told me, even stayed two trees ahead, working hard whether the foreman was not in sight or standing below me. If he were watching me, I probably would have worked harder. The thought never occurred to me to relax once in a while, let the breeze cool off the sweat, or to take it easy climbing up the ladder instead of bounding up. I didn't smoke then so I didn't waste any time rolling one.

After about a week when we were going back to work, Dominguez walked up alongside of me. I knew he was

Dominguez because I had heard that name a lot, especially a little before noon. Somebody would holler, "Dominguez something or other," and this man would mutter and leave the ranch before us. Sometimes he would look up at the sun and check the time on his watch and quietly slip away. It seemed like he was playing a game, trying to leave before the men hollered at him.

"It is hot for you?" Dominguez said.

"Sure is," I said. It was hell going back to work after lunch, the sun burning hot, close above my head. I thought about being at home, sitting in the shade, nibbling on a piece of ice and doing nothing. Going out to the hot orchard, I could only think of being cool and taking it easy. Five more hours seemed like a long time.

"Five hours to eternity," Dominguez said. I looked at him, thinking what a strange thing to say. His face was pockmarked. Many of the men were scarred but this guy's was terrible—ugly pocks under his eyes, on his flat nose, all over his face. And then I noticed he was grinning and I forgot about the marks.

"What do you mean?" I asked

He raised his eyes at me. I was tall for my age. I had done all my growing already. "You are young. Half of the time you do not know what is what." Then wistfully he added, "You are very lucky."

I didn't know what he meant and I kept thinking about it. I didn't exactly resent it but I didn't like it either. Dominguez took the row next to mine and continued talking. He asked where I was born and whether I liked school and things like that. When he asked when I was born I had to think fast.

"That makes you 16 then," he said after I had told him.

"Yeah, that's right," I said, please that I had figured correctly.

"You are not 16."

"Sure I am."

"You are no more than 14. Suppose you can fool the boss, but you cannot fool me," he said.

"How did you know?"

He smiled and shrugged and then changed the position of his

ladder. He talked to me a lot, but I didn't say much, afraid that it would interfere with my work and Dominguez sensed this.

"Trabajo con las manos. I work with my hands," he said, surprising me with Spanish.

"You speak Spanish?" I asked, curious because I had had some Spanish at high school.

"Sure," he said and told me he had gone to Spanish mission school and about how he had to learn everything all over again in English when the Americans came.

We were picking Elberta peaches. They may be the best eating kind but they're the fuzziest too. It was itchy and hot and every time I looked at Dominguez I wanted to scratch myself. It was the heavy sweatshirt he wore, the kind I didn't even wear in winter. Finally, I became too curious and I asked him how he could wear a sweatshirt in the heat.

"This," he said pulling on it, "is the best. Is hot inside and when the wind comes, is cool, that," he said pointing at my glaring white T-shirt, "is too hot." Then still standing in the shade he said, looking up at me on the ladder, "Take it easy boy. You have a long time to live. We all get paid the same. How much you getting anyway?" he said, kidding me.

"Thirty cents an hour," I said. I was told not to tell anyone but by now I was telling Dominguez almost anything. I knew the men were getting thirty-five.

"Thirty cents? That is not right." Then he said something in Tagalog to the men and some looked up and responded.

One Saturday we quit early and I was standing near the bunkhouse waiting for the truck to load up so I could ride to town. Dominguez asked me to come inside and I hesitated.

"What's the matter? You scared?"

"No, I'm not," I said.

Inside the long room was half-dark and the air was a stuffy mixture of sweat, cigar smoke, and strong pomade. One of the men lying on the bunk winked at me. A big fellow who had already taken a bath was slicking back his hair in front of a mirror. He was all dressed up in a purple shirt and suit-slacks hitched up high with short leather suspenders.

"Where you going?" I asked.

"To Sacramento."

"What're you going to do there?"

"Oh, many things," he said. Two or three others said something in Tagalog and they all laughed. I knew they weren't laughing at me, but just the same I didn't know what it was all about.

I followed Dominguez into the kitchen where he had some rice cooking on the kerosene stove.

"The fools go into town every week," Dominguez said shoving a big pan of beans, and lifting his head at me.

"What do you do?" I asked, stringing the beans.

"I stay home and save my money."

"What're you going to do with it?"

"Oh, spend it all at one time," he said, laughing.

Dominguez sliced the beans with a big knife, handling it like a professional cook.

"I'm a good cook. American-style cooking, Chinese-style cooking, any-style cooking. These boys want everything Filipino-style, all in one big pot, just like cooking for hogs," he said, making a face.

"I used to work for a rich American family in Monterey," he continued. It was a nice family. Five years I was there."

"Then you left?"

He nodded. Before I could ask him why, he said, "You would not understand."

"What happened?" I asked anyway.

"The lady was very nice but one day she became, shall we say, too friendly," That's all he said and I tried to guess what he meant while stringing a pile of beans.

I got laid off before the pear season started and I was happy. I didn't care for money. If I had a quarter on Sunday I had a good time; I might go to Roseville to see a movie or go to a local baseball game which didn't cost anything. Father didn't like it when I told him I was let go. He asked me why and I couldn't tell him. I knew I hadn't done anything wrong. I had worked hard, but he wasn't convinced until the boss told him that he had to cut his crew and didn't want to fire any of the Filipinos for fear the whole gang might leave. He also told him that he hated to let me go because I was a good worker, etc., which satisfied father. I didn't get to loaf for very long. When it came to finding work for me, father was a hustler. He took all the money I earned, too. He used it to appease his creditors. He was always worrying over his creditors, cursing them, and I guess I helped him out a little though he never told me so.

Two days later I was working at a big pear ranch.

Fruit season was finally over and I was enjoying my summer vacation when I was sure father couldn't find work for me even if he begged the farmers. I could really take it easy, but school was starting in a week. All summer long I had wanted school to start and now I hated the thought of it.

One day I spotted Dominguez across the street near Stevens Drug Store and I waved to him, calling out his name. He motioned me to come over and I ran across the street. We shook hands and talked like old friends. He had on a chalk-stripe green suit, which I thought was classy. I guess it was a bit loud for a man his age.

"Say, I promised you a treat, remember?" he said.

"Yeah," I said, all smiles.

"Where can we get a milkshake?"

"Over here at Stevens Drug Store," I said eagerly. It was the only place that had a soda fountain.

"Suppose he is all right?" Dominguez asked.

"Sure he's all right. Come on." I led him into the store.

Two women looked at us curiously, but I didn't care. I knew they came to the drug store every day in a different dress for their newspapers or sedatives or whatever. I often wondered if that was all they had to do, drive to town once a day.

We got up on the stools and waited to be served; Mr. Stevens seemed busy chatting with the ladies while we waited. It wasn't that Mr. Stevens didn't know me; sometimes I delivered packages for him and he gave me a choice of a dime or a soda. (Naturally, I took the soda.) Finally, the women left and Mr. Stevens came to wait on us. He glanced at me and then at Dominguez, where his eyes rested for a moment, and shifted back to me.

"A strawberry shake," I ordered, and the druggist lifted the heavy lid of the ice cream compartment and started digging.

"What're you going to have?" I asked Dominguez and he shrugged his shoulders. I watched Mr. Stevens pour milk in the can and I wanted to tell him to take it easy with the milk, I liked it rich and thick.

"Please give me a strawberry milkshake," Dominguez said in his precise English.

The druggist was hooking the can on the shaking machine and his back was turned. "We don't serve any liquor here." It wasn't too clear, but that's what I thought he said. Talking to himself, I supposed. Then he turned around and looking straight at Dominguez he repeated, the words popping out of the corner of his mouth. "We don't serve any liquor here." I didn't know what he meant and I looked at the Filipino. Dominguez didn't look at me. He just handed me a half-dollar and I could feel his palm was sticky. I watched him go out and the green suit didn't look so imposing, the coat drooping loosely over his round shoulders.

Mr. Stevens poured my order in a glass. I still didn't know what happened and, like a dumb kid, I paid and drank the milkshake. I didn't mess with straws; I took it straight from the glass as I had seen others do. I choked. I guess I tried to drink it too fast. The milkshake wasn't as good as I had expected, but I didn't leave any in the glass. I picked up my change and went out.

Dominguez was sitting on a bench, looking at a newspaper. I could tell he wasn't reading because he didn't have his glasses on.

"Thanks a lot, Dominguez," I said, trying to give him the change. He shook his head and lifted his face at me. He did that a lot when he talked and I knew what he meant. "Gee, thanks," I said pocketing the coins.

"How was the milkshake?"

"It was swell," I lied,"but what happened?"

Dominguez didn't look sore, just kind of sad. He was quiet for a moment, then he said, "You mean in there?" indicating with his head. "Oh, I didn't feel like drinking milkshake."

"But," I started to say and he interrupted me. "You know boy, sometimes it is easier for me to get a glass of beer in a saloon."

"I don't know what you mean."

Dominguez winked at me as if to excuse himself for repeating something, "You are young, half of the time you do not know what is what." Then sadly he added, "You are lucky."

I wanted to ask him a few more questions, but the Greyhound bus came and Dominguez picked up his suitcase and boarded the bus without saying anything to me. "So long, Dominguez," I called, waving when I saw him by the window. He grinned. Funny, but I didn't notice the pockmarks on his face, just that sad grin. The bus roared away. I never saw Dominguez after that.

It's been many years now. Too bad I couldn't return Dominguez the treat. He's probably gone by now. Sweet old guy. I haven't been back to Stevens Drug Store in a long time. I know old man Stevens is dead. I wonder if they still don't sell liquor there.

Nihongo Gakko

(Japanese Language School)

The other day I met my friend Jack in Loomis. "We go back a long way, don't we? We used to go to Japanese school together," he said and I was reminded of the carpool our families used to have. Every Saturday morning his father with Jack and his brother in tow would stop by for me on the way to Nihongo Gakko in Penryn. This was convenient but it meant I had to be up and ready and not pretending to be sick. My father would be busy with his work as a fish peddler but by four in the afternoon when school let out he would be there to drive us home.

"Sometimes your father didn't show up and we had to walk," Jack said. I didn't think that that happened too often. Of course, I only had to walk three miles back to Loomis town, while Jack and his brother had three or four more miles to go on the country road and in the winter it would be dark before they got home. I'm sure my father had good reason for not being there, but sorry, Jack.

Our parents went to a lot of trouble so we could learn Japanese. Since we were considered by others to be Japanese and not so much American, they felt we should know the language. So Nihongo Gakko was a common experience for many Nisei. This doesn't mean that we all became proficient; quite the contrary,

Japanese is a difficult language that requires a lot more concentration and dedication than we brought to it. For most of us, Nihongo Gakko was how we spent our Saturdays or after school. Of course we did our required lessons, but it was a less pressurized respite from our regular school. Even our lunches were different; on Saturdays, my mother would pack my lunch of onigiri (riceball) or makizushi (sushi roll) or even leftover okazu (cooked meat and vegetables) and other Japanese things that I wouldn't dare take to American school. But those were lunches that made Saturday school special.

We used to line up outside, standing at arm's length according to grade and height and a monitor would command us to attention—"kiotsuke!"—and then we would bow to the Sensei (teacher) who usually had a few words of greeting, after which the monitor would yell "Susume!" (Forward!) and we would march inside in a fairly orderly fashion.

Since it was a one-room school, Sensei was in charge of many grades and while he attended to one grade the rest of us were expected to study independently which allowed for considerable levity in the classroom and the Sensei constantly warning us to be quiet. But I remember we were on our own a lot and this was difficult, as I already knew my lesson quite well.

I think I had a kind of affinity for the language. I remember when I was about four, even before I could read, I would look at the Japanese section of the *Nichi Bei* newspaper and pick out all the characters with a roof over them and imagine them to be houses somehow connected with people, which actually wasn't too far-fetched.

Depending on the situation, I can say I'm halfway fluent; for a Nisei I think I do pretty well. But after Nihongo Gakko, evening class during high school, advanced class in camp, and a BA in Oriental Languages from UCLA, I should do better. What happened is that I would forget the characters and would have to relearn them. After many repetitions of this process, some of the characters stuck with me, but I am far from literate. As for speaking the language, I wish I could speak "like a native." It's such a pleasure to hear Japanese or any language spoken well. I'd like to live in Japan for a while, preferably in rural Japan where I would hear nothing but Japanese and where I would be forced to speak it constantly. But this is only a dream I have.

Nihongo Gakko was where I picked up the acting bug. Every year there would be a Shugyoshiki, a promotional exercise, where we demonstrated our progress in the use of the language. This would be in the form of stories, songs and dances, providing parents with an evening of entertainment. One year Sensei, who apparently was a frustrated writer, wrote a hilarious comedy skit for our class and the audience roared at everything I said and did on the stage. With that heady sensation and with people telling me how good I was, I began to think I had a talent for acting. (I've been acting off and on ever since.) So my first acting experience was at Nihongo Gakko. I wonder how much Nihongo Gakko helped in our communication with our parents. Most of us could communicate with them on a very basic level—what we learned as children before we began to speak English. Actually, we were needed in their interchange with the hakujin. From the time I was eight or nine, I remember, I was the chief interpreter of the family. Most Issei could carry on a simple conversation about the weather or health or even crops with a hakujin; there would be much laughter to cover blind spots and for good will and it helped that the hakujin spoke in a deliberate pidgin English. But whenever there was a problem (it was usually the hakujin who posed the problem) or a need for some kind of negotiation, there would be a hurried call for me. So there I was a kid of eight or so standing between agitated or certainly anxious adults, one a hakujin, always large and intimidating, and my father or mother or both who didn't quite trust me though they were entirely dependent on me. It was a thankless job, especially when there was tension, then the anger and frustration seemed to come at me from both sides. As a bridge, I was also helping the hakujin, though I was never aware of that. I was only aware of the difference, how big he was, how hairy, how loud and forceful.

By the time I was ten I was also writing business letters for my father, putting down in English what he dictated in Japanese. I would like to see those letters now, though I don't recall that we had any problems with them except for one time. It happened a few years later when I was around fourteen. My father, for some reason that he never made clear to me, had me mail back a postcard advertising a refrigerator showcase. Why he was interested in such a thing was a puzzle to me. It was still the Depression and he was barely making ends meet in the store. I guess he was dreaming; we were expecting something in the mail with pictures of showcases, when one day a dapper-looking hakujin breezed into the store.

"How are you, Mr. Kashiwagi?" he said shaking father's hand. He wanted to know if he had pronounced the name correctly. I translated and father nodded.

"Good, good, Mr. Kashiwagi," he said. Then he asked about our family, even calling me "a fine young man," which almost won me over, I must admit. After extolling the family, he turned his attention to the store. "Fine store, you have here," he said. The store wasn't exactly "fine." With limited funds, father had furnished it with homemade fixtures.

"I'm glad you're buying a showcase from us; it's just the thing that would be perfect right here," he said locating it where the counter was.

I translated this and father said, "Nani?" (What?)

"I've got just the right showcase to put there," he said, now rummaging in his briefcase for some brochures

"Matta, matta," (wait, please), we said.

"Yes?"

"We're sorry but we are not interested in buying a showcase."

Ignoring our comment, he continued, "I'll arrange it so you'll have a beautiful new refrigerator showcase right here within a week. What do you say?"

"Sorry no."

"What's the matter? Are you worried about the payment? Well, don't worry, pay what you can now and the rest you can pay later."

"No, sorry."

"What d'ya mean? No, sorry," he said loudly, suddenly changing his tone. He was no longer the friendly hakujin that I thought he was. "You said you wanted to buy a showcase."

"We never said that."

"I don't understand this at all; you said you wanted to buy a showcase; that's why I came all the way out here from San Francisco."

"No, no."

"What d'ya mean 'No, no'? You are obligated to buy, you know."

I tried to translate this but it was difficult; I was afraid father might explode. Sure enough, before I could finish...

"Deteike!" (Get Out!) he roared, pointing to the door. I didn't have to translate this; the hakujin left hurriedly, barely remembering to take his briefcase. But his parting shot was, "I'll be back." I worried about that though father said it was only a threat; I didn't want to go through another experience like it. But what was worse was when father called me a "Ikujinashi" (coward) and added "Nanimo yaku ni tatan" (good for nothing). I was devastated; I thought I had done the best I could; I didn't realize he was still angry at the hakujin or maybe at himself for having started it all in the first place.

Fusako

She was a special child, adored by everyone. I'm glad I held her often; I can still feel her clinging to me so intensely that I think she knew her life would be brief. But in her three and a half years she brought so much joy to all our lives. I watched her from the very beginning when the doctor and the midwife were there. Of course, we were told to stay away in the other room, but as soon as she was born, we were there to hold her in turn.

She was born in 1933, the year we moved out of the store and the year father was hospitalized. By transposing mother's name "Kofusa," she was named "Fusako." She was not a baby for long, walking long before her first birthday. She warmed the heart of everyone who came in contact with her. Doll-like, she was often made an adorable plaything, tossed from person to person. She was such a good sport; she never protested. I believe she was dropped once and that might have been the cause of the disease that set in. She was exposed to TB, as we all were, but towards the end she developed a slight limp; sometimes we laughed about it, and she laughed along with us. I don't think she was in pain until the very end; when she was in the hospital, tired of the bland food, she asked for a hot dog. It was Sunday and I remember trying to find a market near the hospital for it.

She died of TB meningitis. When mother broke the news to the three of us, we burst into tears and clung to each other, mother included, a rare show of emotion for us. Fusako meant so much to us; she related to each of us in a special way, according to our personalities. A snapshot of her holding a bunch of violets was placed at the altar. Though enlarged and grainy, the photo captured her essential beauty—Fusako holding a bunch of violets is so right. At her funeral, people remarked that she looked like a porcelain doll.

One day I was alone in the bedroom, aroused. I was easily aroused in those days. Mother was busy with a customer in the store. I was about to unzip my trousers when in came Fusako, calling out "Nii-chan" and running towards me. For some reason, I exposed myself in front of little Fusako whose eyes almost popped out of her head. She gasped, turned around and quickly left the room. Instantly, I regretted my action; I expected dire consequences from mother or father or even my siblings but nothing happened. I don't know how it affected Fusako but there was no change in our loving relationship; the incident was to remain our secret. I know it was a terrible thing, a criminal act, but I loved her so much....

Every morning when I said goodbye to her before going off to school, she clung to me, her arms like a vise, her face pressed against mine. When I gently broke away, she waved and called out "Goodbye Nii-chan!" I turned and waved back and she continued to wave and call at the top of her voice. I turned and waved until her calls were faint and I could barely see her waving.

Sixty-five years later, I can still see her waving and calling, "Goodbye Nii-chan!"

Car Dealers
Are Human Too

We had a family friend who used to look in on us and we appreciated his kindness. It was always reassuring to see him, an adult male, if only to know that he was just as confused as we were with the turn of events. It must have taken him some courage to visit us when the man of the house was away, but I know he felt responsible for us and I appreciated his thoughtfulness.

It was early in 1942, when we could still move voluntarily out of the restricted zone, and our friend had decided to move his family. He asked if we would join them. If we did, we would need a car that would accommodate the four of us. We would have to be prepared for any eventuality, he warned—who knows what might happen, we might be attacked, after all we looked like the enemy—a fast getaway car was an absolute necessity. Our pickup, which we used to haul fruit to the fruithouse and for general transportation, would not do. We needed a bigger car, if not a more reliable one.

I pictured being stalled in a strange place, far from a garage or a gas station. Would the people be friendly, would they help us, or would we be run out of town? It was scary; there must be an easier, safer way, I thought. Deep down, I had doubts about going but the man was older and wiser. We decided to join them.

So I went to a car dealer in Roseville about ten miles away and looked at a couple of used cars. One was a forest green Chevy sedan which I thought looked pretty good, though I knew nothing about cars. "It's a good car, runs like a scared rabbit," the dealer said. I took his word and bought it. I remember it belched black smoke, probably using a lot of oil, but it ran fairly well once it got going, even making the climb up to Weimar Sanatorium.

One good thing about the car was that we could all visit father at the hospital, about fifteen miles away. Certainly the pickup would not have made it; sometimes we went by Greyhound bus but never all of us at once. With the Chevy sedan we could go as a family. We made several trips, which proved fortunate, as we would not see father again for nearly four years.

But soon after we bought the car, we were ordered to evacuate so the car became superfluous, another problem to deal with. I went to return the car, which took a bit of determination. I hated this sort of thing but there was no one else to take care of it. I wondered if the dealer would take it back. He had been eager to sell it. "Just leave it and I'll try to sell it for you," he said. That was easy but it wasn't exactly a hopeful sign; I wondered if he was just putting me off. I figured the car was another loss that was quite substantial, as we had paid seven hundred dollars cash.

About a month after we were in Arboga Assembly Center, we were notified of a visitor so I went out to the gate, wondering whom it might be. Earlier, I had had another visitor. Mr. Flynn, the postmaster of Penryn, who had brought us our mail. I had sent him a copy of the camp newsletter and he had commended me for being on the staff.

Any visitor was a welcome sight but on the other side of the fence stood someone. I couldn't believe my eyes—it was the car dealer from Roseville, waving something in the air and looking pleased to see me. A complete stranger before our hurried transaction, he was now an unexpected friend; not only had he kept his word to sell the car but he had taken the trouble to deliver the check. No matter what the amount, his kindness more than made up for the loss which turned out to be less than a hundred dollars. That's when I realized that car dealers are human too, that there are good people even among strangers, even during wartime. He and Mr. Flynn partly made up for the fact that there was no one to see us off when we left our hometown. Actually, there was one person, a Mr. Hayes, and I want to write about him next.

Mr. Hayes

I used to see him across the highway at the fruithouse. He was the manager. He had a mustache. A friendly man, he always called mother "mama" when he stopped by for a pack of Camels. Japanese farmers knew him as Mr. Hayes; those who were familiar with him called him "Chasu" for Chester. Some swore by him while others claimed that they had been cheated by him, even referring to him as a "sonavabitch." He valued the Japanese farmers; through the years they had provided him with quality plums, peaches, and pears which kept the fruithouse in business. What will happen to the fruits? So what if there was a war. Too bad they're being sent away. They're the best farmers. He supposed they would manage without them, though it would be hard. But he'd known them for years; they were his friends. He had drunk their home-brewed sake when he had gone on his round of the farms, even pinched the behinds of some of the mamas who squealed, "Oh, Mistah Hayes!"

We packed most of our things the night before, stuffing our duffel bags and suitcases with bedding, clothes, and the Mason jars of chicken (I'll explain about these in the next sketch), and slept on the floor. Actually, we hardly slept at all that night. The next morning, after a hurried breakfast, we drove ourselves on the pickup to Loomis. I suppose everyone did this, provided their own transportation. We had sold the pickup to our boss for fifty dollars and had arranged to leave it with the Ford dealer in town where the boss would come by for it after we were gone.

Everything was impersonal; we were the unwanted people, being forced out of our homes. The town was quite deserted, windows were shuttered, not a soul was about. We, the "evacuees," as we came to be called, barely greeted each other as we gathered. If we did any more, said anything, we were afraid we would burst into tears. The sight of a pregnant woman only added to the pathos of the moment. Children ran around as children would. The only non-Japanese I remember seeing were the bus driver and the MP when the bus arrived, mercifully breaking up the strangeness and the awkwardness of standing and waiting on the platform of the fruithouse. It was early May and the plums were still quite small and growing on the trees. In a month or so, the platform would be a busy place where packed crates of plums and peaches would be unloaded from the trucks. Now it was a departure point for Japanese and their children being sent off to camp and to an unknown future.

Then we saw Mr. Hayes coming through the crowd, greeting people he knew, wishing them well. "Mr. Hayes, Mr. Chester Hayes is here," everyone said. He looked like he had had a drink or two but it must have taken considerable courage to defy the townspeople, the town itself, to come out to see us off. Even people who hardly knew him rushed forward to shake his hand, more to thank him. You saved the town for us, Mr. Chester Hayes, the town that had been home for most of our lives. We would never forget you, Mr. Hayes. You made our forced departure a little easier.

We left from the fruithouse in May of 1942.

Remembers

the razor blade
remembers
Mr. Stevens the druggist
across the street
should have ripped
off his magazines
other boys did
instead I watched him
come in the morning
overcoat and hat
and leave at night
after shaking the door
all day he dispensed
drugs and sodas
love, hate, shit
what's the difference
while the bus waited
to take us to
concentration camp
he sneered and
wouldn't sell me
the razor blade
remembers

HIROSHI KASHIWAGI. (TULE LAKE, CALIFORNIA, CA. 1944).

Horror Stories

I suppose everyone has horror stories about camp. Mine happened before going to camp. I was 19, the oldest of three children; my father was a patient at Weimar Sanatorium. So, the decision-making responsibility fell on mother and me.

One of the problems was what to do with our chickens. From the original flock of thirty-four, we still had fourteen hens and a rooster. The hens were great layers; we had more eggs than we could use so we would bring them to the store in exchange for groceries. They were large brown eggs that people liked. But what to do with the chickens? Beautiful New Hampshire reds we had raised from day-old chicks we got from a hatchery. We had kept them in an incubator heated by a lantern for about two weeks. Of the fifty chicks, we lost quite a few, perhaps the weak ones, but those that survived grew to be handsome productive chickens. It was foolish to try to sell them. And we didn't want to give them to the boss, why should we? And we certainly didn't want to abandon them as we were leaving most of our furniture.

A few days before evacuation, we decided to butcher them all and it was my chore to take the axe and chop off their heads. I had done this before, singly, but never a whole flock. I tried to be as efficient as I could, a cold, unfeeling machine, hardly breathing. I remember it turned out awkward and messy, a flurry of dust and feathers and blood all over—a lot on my hands. This scene is also in my play *The Betrayed*.

Mother cooked the chickens in shoyu and sugar and packed them in Mason jars that we packed with the clothing in the duffel bags. All those chickens were reduced to about half a dozen jars. At first we enjoyed them in camp, when we weren't used to eating with strangers and the food heaped on tin plates was so unpalatable. At night when we were miserable and hungry, I remember how consoling and comforting the chicken tsukudani was.

The other horror story inspired me to write a play in 1953, *Laughter and False Teeth*, when I was a graduate student at UC Berkeley. It featured a dentist as a villain. When it was performed a few years later, our current family dentist happened to see it and became very upset.

"We dentists are not like that," he said, offended.

I'm sure they are not, but I was writing about a particular dentist who turned out to be a monster. Maybe I exaggerated—but not by much. I based the character on a dentist who treated my mother just before evacuation.

It was late March or early April of 1942, soon after the curfew proclamation that restricted our movements to a radius of five miles from home. We knew we were defying the order when I drove mother to see her dentist in Sacramento, thirty miles away. The dentist determined that mother's teeth were beyond repair and needed to be removed, and because of the curfew he decided to extract them all that very day. I remember sitting in the car waiting for hours. It was late afternoon when mother, with the help of a nurse, finally came out. She looked pale and weak, biting on a large wad of gauze.

"I hope she'll be all right," the nurse said ominously as she saw us off. We drove home without incident and I was vastly relieved that no one had even looked at us suspiciously.

But a few hours later mother began to bleed heavily and she quickly went through all her gauze. Then we tore old bed sheets that she used to stanch the flow that would not stop. Armed with coins, I hurried to a public phone in town and tried calling the dentist. After several attempts, I finally got him.

"My mother's mouth is bleeding badly."

"Have her bite on the gauze dressing I gave her," he said.

"She's done that; she's using old bed sheets now."

"Have her continue biting down on it."

"Will the bleeding stop?"

"Tell her not to move, just keep biting on the dressing. The blood should clot and the flow will stop."

"Are you sure, Doctor?"

There was no answer; he wasn't sure. He hung up.

I rushed home, hoping that the bleeding had stopped; it had not. I told mother what the doctor had said, as if that was going to help. "Be very still, mama," I said. Helpless, I watched for half-hour, an hour, while mother, a strong and determined woman, was now biting on sanitary napkins.

Then suddenly we both remembered that there was a Japanese dentist living in town; he had voluntarily left his home on the coast and was living in our town. We soon found him and he re-sutured the gums, stopping the bleeding. We were so relieved, and grateful to this dentist for saving mother from bleeding to death. I guess the first dentist did what he did because of the curfew and the uncertainty of the times, but he took a huge risk; it was fortunate for everyone that mother didn't die.

But there's more to the story. Mother was always considered an attractive woman. We didn't know that; she was just mom to us but others have told us she was a beautiful person. How humiliating and difficult it must have been for her to go to camp without her teeth, to gum her food in front of all those people in the mess hall. I know she picked up the habit of covering her mouth and not laughing out loud. In time, she learned to live with her condition without losing her self-respect. She also managed to eat without her teeth.

But she never gave up hope of getting her dentures. She made many trips to the dental clinic in camp. She knew that the dentist who had extracted her teeth was at the clinic but somehow she could never see him. Finally, one day they met. She explained who she was and of course he remembered her, though he acted distant and distracted. When she asked about a set of false teeth, he told her brusquely, "Sorry, we aren't allowed to do false plates; beside, I won't be here too long, I'm going in the Army."

Two long years later mother finally had her dentures made by a dental technician. But I was determined that some day I would even the score with that dentist. That is how he turned up in my play as Doctor Yokomichi, a monster of a human being and a caricature of a dentist. It's no wonder that our family dentist was upset.

Assembly Center

T he Greyhound bus took us to Arboga Assembly Center, a temporary camp hastily built on pastureland near Marysville. Leveled over by a bulldozer, it was still a swamp and soon the gnats and mosquitoes began feasting on our warm blood. Though hardly stylish at the time, many women and girls wore pants and slacks out of sheer necessity to protect themselves from the insects. But angry, unsightly welts on legs, arms, necks, even faces were not uncommon. The sight of the barbed-wire fence, the sentry, and the guard towers with searchlights at night was a constant reminder that we were in prison. We had not committed any crime but we were confined, too stunned to question the sudden upheaval in our lives, scrupulously following every order that was handed down.

Reduced to bare essentials, we struggled to adjust to the primitive conditions, waiting in line for meals, holding tin plates, sitting among strangers and eating odd-tasting food prepared by well-meaning but inept volunteer cooks, all fellow evacuees. We ate quickly and left the table, driven by a desire to escape from the situation—but where could we go? It was difficult not to complain and once started there was no end. We must accept the situation, make the most of it, we repeatedly told ourselves.

Our quarters in the tar-papered barrack were a single room

with cots, mattresses, and Army blankets for the four of us. With no furnishings, it was easy to maintain. There were some people we knew but most were strangers. The partitions on both sides of the room did not extend to the top so we could hear everything that went on in the rest of the barrack. Of course, whatever we said or did could also be heard by the others. Privacy was only in the mind; we pretended not to see or hear. Luckily, I was young and able to sleep well enough at night. At least, when I was sleeping, I wasn't aware of our surroundings or situation.

Camp was a great equalizer. Whatever the previous background or status, everyone was an evacuee reduced to a number. It was possible to go in the shower room and run into the president of the Japanese Association or the priest from the temple or the owner of a 40-acre ranch, all people who commanded great respect in our community. In the communal shower room, they seemed so vulnerable and awkward, holding small washcloths over their private parts. Without their clothes it was possible not to recognize them. In fact, that's what we all sought—anonymity, especially in the shower room. I had been trained to bow and greet people, especially adults, but the question was, do I or do I not? Should I or should I not? A touchy, difficult problem of ethics in the shower room, standing buck naked, avoiding eye contact, trying to cover our embarrassment. Those of us who had been to high school were used to communal showers, but it must have been agonizing for the older folks to be so open among people of all ages, especially youngsters who took delight in staring at others.

There was a shallow three-foot square pool at the entrance to the shower room that everyone ignored and jumped over; it was supposedly filled with a disinfectant to prevent athlete's foot. We soon learned the best protection against athlete's foot was to wear a pair of geta (wooden clogs) which kept our feet several inches off the concrete floor. Of course, they would have to be made from scrap lumber so I didn't have mine until many months later when we were in Tule Lake. Meanwhile, I jumped over the disinfectant pool and took my chances.

What was most outrageous was going to the latrine: a public outhouse with accommodations for eight or eight holes in a line without partitions between them. How disconcerting it was, sitting there cheek by jowl, this necessary and what should have been a regular and fairly pleasurable function. An oft-heard remark in the latrine was: "Erai toko de deaimasu neh!" which might be translated as, "What a place to be meeting" or "What an ungodly place to meet" or "What a miserable situation we find ourselves in."

I tried going early in the morning or late at night but others had the same idea. I solved the problem, at least for myself, by volunteering to work at the hospital where I could use the facilities there in relative privacy. The flush toilets must have been connected to a septic tank.

After graduating from high school in Los Angeles I had returned home to work on the ranch. We were sharecropping a fruit orchard, getting an advance of $50 a month; of course, we couldn't live on that, so after our harvest we went to pick grapes in Lodi for two or three months. I was waiting for my brother to graduate and take over the ranch work so I could go to college. In 1942 when he was a senior and about to graduate, we were sent to camp. So there went my college hopes, at least for then.

But in camp I was restless and eager to advance myself. As a staff member of the camp newsletter I put out an appeal for people interested in drama, hoping to attract someone from whom I could learn acting. But the notice brought no response, making me feel like an oddball. Was I the only one interested in theater? We were all from small towns; was theater for white folks only?

I wrote to my former teacher asking her for help in forming a drama group. I had been a star student in her public speaking class. She also taught drama, directing plays that I had seen performed. I was hopeful that I would hear from her. It was naïve of me to think this way. Not only did she not reply, but I learned later that she was an active leader of an anti-Jap faction in the community. It was hard to accept that a teacher of mine, someone I had great respect for, would be such a bigot. Chalk one against America, sadly and painfully. One of many betrayals.

My work as an orderly at the makeshift hospital included giving back rubs to patients, servicing urinals and bedpans, taking temperatures, giving bedbaths, preparing the late evening snacks and serving them, changing bandages, and other chores. I once had to change the bandage, daily, of someone who had had a hemorrhoid operation. I learned it was a painful operation, especially the healing process, and I hoped I would never have to go through it myself. I also prepared a middle-aged patient for an appendectomy, shaving off his pubic hair. When I had finished shaving him, the patient who had been very understanding of my nervousness and very cooperative for his own protection, I suppose, said, "Thank you for making me a young boy again."

In white uniforms and lab coats, the hospital people all looked glamorous, acting like nurses, lab technicians and doctors engaged in noble work. Actually there were precious few professionals, but the highest aspiration of many Nisei, especially those who excelled in school, was to become a doctor. I was no exception. Working as an orderly and observing the nurses and doctors, however, I decided that medicine as a profession was not for me. This realization would come later when I worked at the hospital in Tule Lake.

During the two months at Arboga we heard numerous rumors that we would be sent to another camp. This was the first of the many rumors that would plague us in the next three to four years that we would be in camp. Finally, we got word that we would be moved to Tule Lake in Northern California. As a barrack monitor (I had volunteered for that), I was now assigned to be car monitor on the train. My principal task was to pass out the lunch of sandwiches and milk to the passengers and baby food to the mothers of infants—there were a few in our car—and to caution everyone from peeking out of the shaded windows. It was a most uncomfortable all-night trip in an ancient milk train that had not been used in years. I'm sure few were able to sleep on the hard wooden benches; grim-faced and uncomplaining, we completed the trip without incident, much to my relief. For most, this was a rare, perhaps even their first, train ride but there was no sign of any levity, joy or spirit of adventure among the "passengers" that I could see.

Tule Lake

When we arrived at Tule Lake in the morning, we were greeted by a man who claimed to be our Block Manager. It was nice to have someone welcome us on our arrival at this desolate place near the northern border of California. "If you need anything, just ask me," he said. He provided us with mattresses and Army blankets; we unpacked and settled in.

After the miserable experience in Arboga, we were excited about the flush toilets in the latrines. In fact, we made a special trip to the latrine to check them out—two rows of porcelain toilets that actually flushed. We tried it several times to see if they really worked; they did. However, the lack of partitions between the toilets and the trough urinals for the men were a bit disconcerting.

One of the first things I did was to look for work. I took the first available job as a carpenter's helper putting up sheet rock in the apartments. I joined a motley crew of five or six men of disparate ages. I believe I was the youngest among them. Except for the crew chief, none of us had had much experience as a carpenter. Some were barely able to hit a nail straight, but we were welcomed everywhere as daiku-san (carpenters). People moved out all their furniture (crude tables and chairs, hastily made from scrap lumber) and waited for us to finish the job. I remember we were served sodas and refreshments and treated rather royally, which to me was embarrassing. I thought we were just doing a job, making the quarters livable, finishing what the government had failed to do.

The searchlights at night were eerie. Many of the soldiers in the guard towers were recent transfers from the war in the South Pacific, young, nervous, and trigger-happy. We didn't dare go near the fence for fear of being shot at; there were tragic instances of that. But aside from the physical confinement, there was the invisible fence enclosing our spirit. This imprisonment of the spirit, the psychological effect, even more than the actual fence, was to be the most ravaging part of the camp experience, leaving a scar that would remain with us for the rest of our lives.

I was determined to make the best of the situation. I attended classes in sociology and public speaking that were taught by recent students at UC Berkeley and other colleges. I went to the library and checked out books to read. I remember reading John Steinbeck's *The Grapes of Wrath*, a novel I enjoyed and identified with; I had met some of the "Okies" that Steinbeck wrote about. And, of course, I was familiar with fruit picking and life in the labor camps.

Then there was an item in the *Tulean Dispatch*, the camp newspaper, calling for people interested in acting to form a little theater, and I found my home. I was to spend most of my non-working hours with the theater group. I learned acting by actually performing on stage in front of an audience. That was heady and soon I was playing lead parts.

We presented a program of three one-act plays that we performed every night for about two weeks. The plays were all American plays with Caucasian characters. We, inmates of a prison for Japanese, were ironically portraying Caucasian characters—and our audience loved it. I think we, the performers as well as the audience, were only interested in theater: the curtain, the lights, the actors, the make-believe. Actually, we had no choice, because there were no plays about Japanese Americans. No one was writing original plays; that was to come much later after the war.

I remember playing a righteous cleric with a turned-back collar in a comedy that was great fun. I also played a dream-maker in a fantasy about a romance between Pierrot and Pierrette, wearing a large, ungainly hat. My most notable role was as a condemned prisoner meeting his execution, spouting lines from Shakespeare about "cowards die many times before their death; the valiant but once." The play was *The Valiant*. I had to smoke in the part so I rehearsed handling a cigarette. That probably started my smoking habit. I heard that some of my friends came just to watch me smoke on stage.

I also joined a writers club. I think we met weekly. Most of the members were college students, either from Cal or UCLA. To me, a mere high school graduate and a country kid at that, everyone seemed highly educated and sophisticated. I knew I didn't belong with them, but my interest in writing drew me to the club. Feeling small and inadequate, I sat quietly, watching and listening to the proceedings. Everyone was encouraged to write something and read it to the group for comments and criticisms. Not everyone wrote; many were observers. Those who wrote were writing about life before camp—city life, college life, both new to me. Some wrote fiction in the manner of the hard-boiled detective genre or in the Dos Passos or Hemingway style. It all sounded great and everyone was impressed. I was too. Thinking back, the writing wasn't so hot. In fact, it was pretty bad—often sophomoric. No one in the group that I know was a writer or became one. I think a few became scholars.

I wrote a story that was based on something that happened just before evacuation. It was autobiographical, hand-written, about a country boy longing for a radio and finally one day taking the Greyhound bus to Sacramento and buying a small Zenith radio. What a thrill that was—a brand new radio, all his own, that played loudly and clearly, especially at night. But he didn't get to enjoy it for long because of the war and evacuation. I don't remember what happened after that....I'm sure he took the radio to camp...maybe it stopped playing. I remember the story was titled "The Zenith Radio." As I finished reading the story, I expected some reaction but there was none, just silence. Why didn't they say something? Did they not like it? I have wondered why they didn't say anything. Did they resent the fact that this young country hick had shown them up, had written a story that moved them or was the story too close to home? I decided it wasn't much of a story. Later, the leader of the club wanted to publish the story and asked me for it but by then I had thrown it out. I realize now that I missed a rare opportunity as the *Tulean Interlude*, a magazine collection of writings done in Tule Lake camp, became a primary source for scholars. It is deposited in the Bancroft Library at UC Berkeley, along with other camp documents.

I was having the time of my life, working a few hours a day as a dishwasher in the mess hall and devoting the rest of my time to what I loved—acting, reading, writing and meeting people with similar interests. Camp life was great. But it all came to an abrupt end in February 1943 with the so-called "loyalty registration," which was a joint order by the Army and the WRA to facilitate the Army in recruiting volunteers and the WRA in moving us out of camp. All male and female internees seventeen and older were ordered to answer a series of questions in a "Statement of United States Citizenship of Japanese Ancestry," of which the key questions were questions 27 and 28:

> *No. 27: Are you willing to serve in the armed forces of the United States on combat duty wherever ordered?*
>
> *No. 28: Will you swear unqualified allegiance to the United States of America and faithfully defend the United States from any or all attack by foreign or domestic forces, and forswear any form of allegiance or obedience to the Japanese Emperor, to any other foreign government, power or organization?*

We refused to register. At the beginning most of the people at

Tule Lake were against the registration order. Confused over the questions, we went around to see what the others were doing. In our family, the decision became unanimous; mother's primary concern was to keep us together. Her great fear was that if we registered, we would be forced out of camp and drafted by the Army. If my father had been with us, I don't know what we would have done, what his decision would have been. I know it would have been much easier for us; he would have made the decision and we would either follow it or not.

My position was this—why was I, an American citizen, thrown in prison without cause, without due process? Why were they questioning my loyalty? I was an American, a loyal American. If they restored my status as a rightful citizen, let me go free, out of this prison, I would do anything required of me. Why should I answer the ambiguous questions? I would follow my conscience and refuse to register.

To underscore the compulsory nature of the registration, we were warned that non-compliance was a violation of the Espionage Act with penalties of twenty years in prison, a $10,000 fine or both. The Project Director with Army officers came to key mess halls and read off names of draft-age men expected to register.

Block 42, a neighboring block, was one of the first blocks ordered to register. Most of the young men there had signed up for repatriation to Japan. That was ironic, as they were all citizens of this country. As a reprisal, the Administration picked them first to register. When no one appeared at the block office on the designated day, the authorities took action. Around 5 o'clock in the afternoon, the mess bells rang out urgently and alarmingly, announcing the arrival of the soldiers to round up the recalcitrant evacuees. The young men who already had their suitcases packed were forced at bayonet point onto the Army truck. Everyone was outraged and emotions ran high. Mothers, girlfriends, brothers and sisters were tearfully bidding goodbye to the young men who were being taken to the county jail outside of camp. This show of force by the Administration was meant to break down our resistance, but it only hardened our resolve. We returned to our apartment to pack our bags and wait to be taken away.

But the Block 42 men were soon released because the WRA had no cause to hold them. We continued to resist and nothing happened. Years later, I was devastated to read that the registration order had not been compulsory, that there was nothing compelling us to register: a fact that the Administration never disclosed to us. To this day, many Nikkei believe that the order had been compulsory. Furthermore, the threat of 20 years in jail and/or $10,000 fine for non-compliance had been just that: threats. Laboring under these conditions, fearful and uncertain, we refused to register. As a consequence, we were held at Tule Lake when it became Tule Lake Segregation Center. And we became known as the infamous "No-No Boys."

I didn't know what my fate would be. I was hopeful that nothing drastic would happen. I had no intention of going to Japan. Since they would not release me, I was going to sit out the war in camp. I just wanted to be who I was—a Japanese American, an American of Japanese descent, an American. Obviously, I was not pro-Japan even though I could read and write Japanese; I was more advanced in Japanese language than those who were hastily trained at the military language schools were. With my language skill I realize I could have been very useful to my country. I could have served in the Military Intelligence Service as many Kibei and Nisei did with great distinction. If only my country had been more fair and trusting....

But renunciation was another thing. When I heard talk of it, I felt it was only for pro-Japan fanatics; certainly, not for me. I tried not to concern myself with it. I didn't think it would happen to me, but it did. Unknowingly, I was swept into it, succumbing to the pressure—both outside and within our own family. I was influenced by a family friend whose wife and children were in Japan and who was planning to join them after the war; it was natural for him to be pro-Japan. He came over every day; I tried not to listen to him but I guess he was an influence. Though I didn't agree with him, I didn't want to defy him; I was lazy; I didn't want to think; I didn't want to confront the problem and make a decision; to put my foot down and assert my real feelings. I thought it would just go away. For my refusal to face reality, I was to pay dearly.

Then one day my brother forced the issue. "Are we Americans or are we Japanese? Let's make it clear." I gave in.

Renunciation was totally unnecessary. We had already made our protest known by not registering. To give up our citizenship was stupid and redundant. I always thought that I had brought it on myself but actually it wasn't my fault at all; the government had accommodated us by passing a special legislation, making it easy for us to renounce and we fell for it. Again I was betrayed, not only by the fanatics who agitated for it, but also by my own government for willingly allowing it.

After I was released in early March of 1946, I realized for the first time that during the three and a half years I had done nothing to further myself. What had I done? Well, I played a lot of card games—hours of pinochle—so much so that today I can't stand to look at cards. The picnic tables in the mess hall left me with a permanent aversion for them, even at picnics. What else? I learned to smoke; this was at a time when cigarettes were scarce and we went around mooching off one another. After fifteen years I struggled to give up the habit. I didn't even get married. I should have married and started a large family at government expense, but I guess I was a bit young. So for three and a half years, I was just existing, vegetating, enduring, surviving and hanging on to...to what? To my sanity...something I would never admit.

I lost all initiative to do anything new or daring, sticking to the familiar daily routine. Why? I think I was barely hanging on. If I took a moment to think, wavered from my routine, I think I would have fallen apart. I guess this is what it's like to be incarcerated. Playing baseball with others like myself helped while I was involved in the game but after it was over it was back to bleak, numb reality.

I feel I have paid many times over for the position I took at Tule Lake. Certainly, you don't go around telling people you spent time at Tule Lake during the war. You try to push that back somewhere and not think about it; you try to block out that part of your life, but you have to live with it. You try to find a niche in society and hope that no one will pry into your past.

Living under such pressure, it's inevitable that there should be doubts and questions about your actions and feelings of guilt. Did I do something bad or wrong? If the circumstances were to be repeated, how would I act? I would take the same position I took as a young man back in 1943. Only this time, there would be no doubt, no hesitation, and no confusion. I would have the advantage of hindsight and I would definitely protest, no matter what the cost.

HIROSHI KASHIWAGI AS MANAGER OF BLOCK 40.
(TULE LAKE, CALIFORNIA, CA. LATE 1945)

The Block Manager's Canary

I knew three block managers in camp—actually, four, as I was one myself. Though I don't consider myself a regular block manager, since I served only a few months toward the end of camp when there was little administrative work. But recently a former resident of my block unnerved me by announcing to one and all, "He was our Block Manager!"

I didn't know how to take that. A block manager was indeed an important functionary in the block. He was the administrative head of 250 to 300 persons; he was responsible for the smooth operation of the block; he was a mediator in the event of a dispute among the residents; and he was the chief liaison with the Administration. But for all that, he was not always the most popular or the most respected person in the block. In fact, he was often called "blockhead" behind his back.

Other duties of the block manager, many of which he delegated to his "lazy" secretary (I know because I was a secretary to two block managers) included distribution of the mail. This was one of his more pleasant tasks, as people associated him with mail and of course everyone loves mail, no matter where they are. People looked forward to the mail car every day. When it arrived, they flocked to the block office and watched eagerly while the block manager carefully inspected each piece of mail before sticking it in the right pigeon hole. Only after he was through with the entire pile would he hand over the letter or newspaper or whatever to the proper addressee.

The block manager also issued passes; helped residents when they were ill (for example, summoning the ambulance in an emergency), conducted surveys of which there were too many (I was given this task so I know); reported repairs to the proper department; issued light bulbs; sent in requisition for coal delivery; and made sure that the toilet paper in the latrines did not run out. But his most important duty, the very reason for his existence as far as the administration was concerned, was attending the weekly block managers' meeting. This was of course obligatory and most block managers took it quite seriously—some, in fact, too seriously, to the extent of putting on a necktie before going to the meeting.

Ostensibly, the meeting was a venue for the block managers to discuss various issues and report the feelings of the residents, airing any grievances. But in fact, the block managers had little or no voice in the scheme of things. The Administration's primary interest was to see that the block managers clearly understood their directives that they would then convey to the residents. In that sense, the block manager was not much more than a messenger and a convenient tool of the Administration.

During mealtime he would use a spoon and tap on a coffee mug to gain attention and announce the latest directive from the Administration to a somewhat disinterested and often put-upon group of diners.

I knew, as I've said, several block managers. First, there was the one who greeted us when we first arrived at Tule Lake. After a miserable all-night train ride, it was nice to have anyone welcome us. But I was a smart-alecky nineteen-year-old, suspicious of any authority figure. I wondered why this guy, who looked to be a Nisei, though a complete stranger, kept saying, "I'm your Block Manager" and telling us what to do. Well, I learned later that as part of the early contingent, he had had access to the so-called "cushy" jobs and because of his supposed bilingual ability, he was hired as a block manager and assigned to our block. I thought that his Japanese, when he made his mess hall announcements, was rather stiff and textbook-like, and his English wasn't much better. As I suspected, he turned out to be a rather cold, pompous and officious person and I never had much to do with him. During the loyalty registration he and his family were the first to move out, leaving behind his elderly parents.

The other two block managers I knew better, since I worked for them as a secretary. There was Mr. Handa, an older man, a well-educated Issei. Before becoming a block manager, he had been a warden. I remembered seeing him in a dark uniform complete with a cap, a badge, a nightstick and leggings. Now, as a block manager, he looked more like a teacher, the Japanese language school teacher that he was before the war. Still, his mustache and stern demeanor always reminded me of a Prussian general. Actually, he was an easygoing man who didn't take his position too seriously; he had a curious habit of putting his feet up on the desk. That's the kind of person he was. He let me do pretty much as I pleased, which was okay by me. He was a block manager for less than a year until he left camp, when I succeeded him. But before Mr. Handa was Mr. Sumitomo.

Mr. Sumitomo became the block manager almost by default. When the first manager and his wife, who was also his secretary, left abruptly, the positions of block manager and secretary became vacant. Two concerned block elders took it upon themselves to try to convince some people from within the block to take over, but no one was interested. That's when Mr. Sumitomo, in a spirit of altruism, came forward. "I got no schoolin,' no qualification and I got no business even thinkin' about it but we gotta have a block manager, no? I'll be block manager and you be secretary," he said with such finality that I said okay before I realized what I was doing. I guess I was taken by his spirit and I kind of liked the man. Anyway, that's how we became a team of sorts.

Mr. Sumitomo always wore a hat. He was from Hawaii; he told me he was born in Hanapepe. Though he said he had no schooling, I knew he had been to high school. But he sure was hard on himself. "Mine too small," he would say, referring to his penis. Now, why would he say that? He was no smaller than most guys were.

I really liked the announcements he used to make in the mess hall. I think the diners didn't mind the interruptions either. His mixture of simple, almost childlike Japanese and Hawaiian pidgin English always seemed to amuse and charm them. But funny or not, Mr. Sumitomo was totally serious.

I guess I wasn't much help to him. As a secretary I swept and mopped the office floor every morning, I sorted the mail when Mr. Sumitomo was away or busy. I made out requisitions as needed and I did whatever he asked me to do. What else was there? Sure, I had plenty of time to sit out front with my friends and smoke our homemades and watch the girls go by. I must confess that we undressed each of them mentally and embarrassed them so much that they held on to their dresses as they hurried by. "More bettah play cards inside, heh, Mr. Sumitomo?"

I heard Mr. Sumitomo was complaining about me to the others. "He too lazy, don't do nottin, play cards alla time." Yes, we did play a lot of cards. But I wasn't into cards; it was just a game. I thought I was doing my duty keeping the fellows occupied. We played pinochle for hours on end, so much so that I have never played it since camp. Recently, I read in *The New Yorker* that "to play pinochle" is a euphemism for "being a philanderer." I thought that was interesting.

Mr. Sumitomo had some odd quirks, one of which was to keep a canary in a cage. This was puzzling to me, considering our situation, but it was his business so I didn't question him about it. Maybe he needed a diversion, a pet. He always seemed to be stressed and unhappy. Maybe he was overextended or maybe the job was getting to him. It was, after all, thankless, frustrating work. Anyway, he always appeared in the morning puffy-faced and grim-looking; it was never a good morning with him.

One day, however, he was really sick with a sinus infection

and had to go to the hospital. He asked me if I would look after his canary and of course I told him "sure, don't worry." It was simple enough feeding and watering the bird, but one day I got careless and forgot to close the little gate to the cage and the canary was gone.

Now, Mr. Sumitomo was one of those people who re-cooked his food to suit his taste. He would bring his plate of food from the mess hall and cook it again on his hot plate; once he invited me to eat and offered me what was famously called "slop suey." He had cooked it again using hard candy in place of sugar. Imagine finding little white pellets of hard candy in the slop suey. To wash the dishes and utensils, he always kept a bucket of water handy.

Frantically, I looked around the room for the canary, then I saw something in that bucket. "No!" I remember saying to myself. Well, it was the bird, lifeless. I picked it out of the water and slapped it a few times, trying to revive it. I guess I felt responsible for its death.

When Mr. Sumitomo came home from the hospital, of course, I had to tell him about the canary. I was quite contrite and even admitted that I might have been careless.

"Don't worry; no can help," he said, much to my relief.

It was soon after that that Mr. Sumitomo announced that he was quitting as block manager, that the job was making him sick. Maybe that was true, but I knew that he had other concerns. Once he had told me that he had a family in Japan, a wife and two kids in Hiroshima.

In February 1946, Mr. Sumitomo was one of 4,406 Tule Lake inmates who voluntarily left for Japan. When I went to see him off, he was barely recognizable because he was wearing three hats, one on top of the other, and extra clothing under his brown suit. That was the last time. Mr. Sumitomo and the others had gone to a country that had been totally devastated. I don't know whether he got to see his wife and children in Hiroshima. Some time later I heard that he was working as an interpreter for the Army occupation.

Anyway, I wrote a story about it for a Japanese language class and the instructor read it to the class: how the canary escaped and drowned and how it affected me. But I didn't explore how or why the bird fell in the water. Was it deluded by its own image in the water? Could be. Was it thirsty? How could that be? I had given it water every day. Cooped up in a cage, was it so unused to flying that even when given a chance to fly, it couldn't—and, like a faulty plane, it had failed mid-flight? Now, that's a good possibility.

Radio Station KOBY
in Medford, Oregon

Daytime we could get only two radio stations —
small town stations in Medford and Klamath Falls,
Oregon that played incessantly.

the women dug the lakebed
and turned up seashells
long dormant in the sand
sorted and cleaned
painted and shellacked
they became ornamental things
trinkets and necklaces
made in captivity
    this is Radio Station KOBY in Medford, Oregon

we took pieces of 2 x 4
whittled and carved them
mine were unremarkable
but old Yoshimoto-san
always did women
a shelf lined with them
severe and woodbound
more Egyptian than Japanese
all frontal and nude
    this is Radio Station KOBY in Medford, Oregon

baloney, hot and frothy
on the metal platter
they said it was horse meat
we ate it anyway
even made sandwiches
with mustard and mayonnaise
we rolled Bull Durhams
watched the girls
did nothing mostly
while we smoked
our homemades
      this is Radio Station KOBY in Medford, Oregon

we liked to shower
in summer and winter
standing in wooden clogs
didn't want to get athlete's foot
turned on the hot and cold water
what a pleasure that was
but often they ran out of coals
then we couldn't shower
we watched for smoke
from the furnace chimney
counted the days
we hadn't showered
missed our showers
wanted to feel clean
      this is Radio Station KOBY in Medford, Oregon

what's that old fart
doing in the shower room again?
copping looks at our genitals
okay creep
look all you want
there's no charge
but don't tell me
to shave my head
join the Hoshi-dan
become a fanatic Japanese
I'm here in protest
I am an American
want to be treated like one
I repeat
I am an American
naked as I am
so creep
get the hell out of my sight
    this is Radio Station KOBY in Medford, Oregon

he was killed for no reason
just driving a farm truck
past the gate
ordered to get out
he did
and he was shot
by a nervous white boy soldier
we went to his funeral
thousands did
the whole camp almost

only our respect for the dead
held back our anger
sitting or standing
we bent the Tules
growing in the firebreak
    this is Radio Station KOBY in Medford, Oregon

So, you were in Tule Lake, huh?
Yeah.
I was there too.
Oh?
But I relocated early...to Chicago.
That so?
What did you do?
I stayed back.
You stayed, huh?
Go ahead ask it.
What?
I know you want to.
Oh, we don't have to talk about it.
It's all right, go ahead.
Were you a...no-no boy?
That's right.
Heard you guys had trouble.
Some.
How long were you there?
You mean in prison?
Well...you know what I mean.

Three years ten months.

That long, huh?

Yep.

This is Radio Station KOBY in Medford, Oregon

So you goin' to the Tule Lake reunion?

Nah.

You know about it, don't you?

Yeah, I heard.

Why aren't you goin' then?

Not interested.

Guess I'll go.

Oh sure.

There'll be singin' and dancin'.

Like ole times, huh?

That's right, partyin' and dancin', remember?

Check out the women?

Well...forty, fifty years...

Never too late, huh?

That's right. Hubba, hubba.

Jitterbug?

Might give it a whirl.

Well, don't go breakin' your balls.

Say, why don't you come along?

Nah.

Hell, it's been forty, fifty years, water under
    the bridge, huh?

No sucker, not for me.

This is Radio Station KOBY in Medford, Oregon

A Trip to Cedarville

*I*t was near the closing of camp, when restrictions were being relaxed a bit, that I heard from our neighbor George about Mr. Crane, the Camp Reports Officer, taking a small group to entertain some high school students at Cedarville. Cedarville is in Modoc County, about 120 miles from Tule Lake. George and a few of his musician friends were going and he asked me if I would be interested in joining them. My first thought was "I don't sing or play an instrument, what could I do?" George said they wanted someone to provide some comic relief and he thought that maybe I could tell stories. Stories? What stories? Certainly not about camp to white high school kids who probably never saw any Japanese in their life before, living in a small town in Northern California, probably very conservative. It was around November 1945, not long after the end of the war. We were hearing of the "No Japs" signs up in our hometown, and of dynamiting of barns, even the burning down of the home of a 442nd veteran. But the chance to go outside was terribly appealing. I would do anything for that, even make a fool of myself if I had to. After being cooped up for almost four years, the thought of being free again was over-powering. I had to go. I told George sure, I was more than willing to go, and I'd find something to do to make my going purposeful.

I quickly looked through some magazines that were in the

block office in search of jokes. I found a few that struck me as being funny without being off color, some with even a bit of wit. I memorized them, so that they were a part of me, before joining the group early one morning. The car was loaded down with Mr. Crane, who drove, and the five of us plus various musical instruments. I believe there was a violin, a saxophone, an ukulele, and an electric guitar. First we stopped in the town of Tulelake; I think Mr. Crane stopped for us so we could experience being out of camp. So this was how it felt to be free. It was indescribable; we couldn't help rushing around. We didn't care if we attracted strange looks from the townspeople; and in fact we probably did, but we were too busy to notice, running in and out of the stores. At one store, which I believe was a drug store, I made a big purchase of a pack of Wrigley spearmint gum. What a thrill that was.

Back in the car we continued on our trip. Though crowded, it was great to be riding in a car, a passenger car, going miles and miles away from camp. We went through Alturas, the county seat of Modoc County, and finally arrived at Cedarville, which was at the foot of a mountain close to the California/Nevada border. It was around 11 o'clock. The students were all seated in the classroom, awaiting our arrival. They seemed curious to see us, but were warm and welcoming. I'm sure they had been well briefed about us: that it was an accident of war that we were confined in the camp at Tule Lake, that we were just as American as they were.

I noticed that some of the students were sitting together as if on a movie date, the boys with their arms around their girlfriends. After a few words of welcome by the principal, the program began, and the musicians played several numbers. Recently, I asked Ed, who played the ukulele, what he remembered of the trip. After more than 50 years, he remembered some things I didn't and I remembered some things he didn't. He thought they played some Hawaiian songs. I remembered a violin solo, but he wasn't sure of that. The audience was very enthusiastic; they acted like they had never heard live music before. Maybe they hadn't.

Then I was introduced. I was the only one speaking directly to them. I said that since I couldn't sing or play an instrument, I would tell some jokes and I heard a murmur go around the room. Even as I was telling the first joke, I wondered how it would go over. I believe the jokes had to do with little Audrey—rather silly jokes, I'd be embarrassed to tell them now. But much to my surprise and delight, the audience roared from the very first joke which energized me to tell all the jokes that I had prepared and I had them literally rolling in the aisles. Were the jokes that good? Was I that much of a comedian? Who knows? But it was exhilarating and memorable. After the program was over, the kids gathered around us to tell us how much they had enjoyed it. I think they wanted to get a closer look at us, make sure they were actually seeing what they were seeing. Some even offered to give us a tour of their school.

Then we were taken through the town to a little restaurant where the local Lions Club had their weekly meeting. Here, we were served lunch with the club members, most of whom were fathers of the kids at the high school we had just visited. I don't remember what we had to eat; nothing remarkable, though it was cattle country. At any rate, they had heard of the great impression we had made at the high school, so they were all very warm and friendly. After lunch we repeated our program. Again I went through my joke routine for the club members, some of whom looked a little lost without their horses. Most were cattle ranchers but there were some storekeepers and a few professionals. I swear they laughed at my jokes even louder than the kids had earlier. I could tell the men were having a rip-roaring time, slapping their thighs; I'm sure they had had something to drink by then. But how they could laugh.

When we returned to camp, it was already past suppertime in the mess halls. Mr. Crane invited us to have dinner at his place. He had bought some steaks in Cedarville and now Mrs. Crane prepared them for us with lots of potatoes smothered in onions. "What a treat this is!" we all exclaimed. "You earned it," Mr.

Crane said, pleased with us for having done a good public relations job. The steak dinner, our first in over three years—what a fitting ending it was to a trip that we would remember for the rest of our lives.

Free Streets

*I*t was in March of 1946, the morning after my brother, sister and I came out of camp. We had been given $25 each and a free ride on the train. The train seemed better than the old milk train with the shade drawn which had taken us to Tule Lake in 1942. After being held until almost the closing of camp, we were finally released. I guess we were used to being confined, but camp was nearly deserted. We were beginning to wonder when, if ever, we would be given the notice to leave. Mother was already out and living with two other families in Loomis. We would join her there.

It seemed like a brand new day in Sacramento when we got off the train. As we walked the once-familiar streets, the air was so clear and pure that I wanted to drink it. The pristine clarity of everything in the sunlight—the trees, the flowers, the lawns, the houses, the cars moving in traffic, the people going about their lives—was like seeing the world for the first time. Voraciously, I tried to take it all in, through the pores of my skin, deep inside, for replenishment, for nourishment, for renewal. So this was the outside world that we had longed for.

Being free, I was suddenly hit with the thought that I had spent the past four years of my life in prison where time had stopped. I too had slowed to a standstill, trying to shield myself so I wouldn't go out of control, enduring day to day, not thinking, just vegetating. There had been no cells of course, only the barbed-wire fence and the guard towers that were confining enough, both physically and spiritually. I would carry the psychological scars for the rest of my life.

And then we saw him coming toward us, someone familiar, another Japanese American, a comforting sight. He had been at Tule Lake and had gotten out a few months before us. Of course, we knew him. I had known him in the Young Buddhist Association. He had on striped overalls, looking like he was employed at a fish market or a grocery store. He was pushing a hand truck. We were ready to stop him and say hello and we expected him to greet us too, even welcome us to the outside. But as he approached us, he looked away and walked around us as if he didn't know us at all and we were stunned, standing there with our hands in midair, our hellos caught in our throats, and our mouths ajar, wondering what the hell happened.

Hey, we just came out of camp, a little late, yes, but we're here, out of that hellhole and you were there too until a few months ago. What's going on? What's with this act, anyhow?

So this is the outside world. Reality. What a rude awakening.

Oh, I see. Camp was camp, it was a different situation and now that you're outside starting over again, you want to put the camp behind you, forget that life. You don't want anything that reminds you of it, people like us, people you met there, friends you made… what friends? Friend, ole boy. So we gathered from different places, from different schools, and we met. That's what happened to all of us. And now you choose not to know me, pretend you never did, like we were never in camp? Are you sure you want it that way? It's a small world, you know and you just might regret it some day. OKAY, if that's how you want it, I hope I never see you again; right, you piece of shit!

Of course, through the years, our paths would cross, though I tried to avoid him as much as possible. When he was starting in business and needing all the advantages, I heard he was telling an acquaintance that he knew me. What people will do to get ahead; I could not believe it. On rare occasions, when we met face to face and said hello, I said it grudgingly. He must have gotten the message; it was clear enough how I detested him and why.

I know that forgiveness is a noble virtue, but it's not one that I've been able to cultivate easily. I've tried, but it seems to get in the way of being true to myself. Being true to myself, maybe that's my problem. At any rate, I don't think the person in question was worth the trouble.

The incident is especially vivid in my memory because it happened when I was most vulnerable—when, after nearly four years in the dark, I was feeling my way in the light, when even a nod or a smile would have been welcome enough, would have meant so much. Instead, rejection like a dash of cold water, more like a slap across my face.

The rejection, sometimes overt but often subtle, was to shadow me through the years. When I was with other Japanese Americans, I tried not to talk about camp, but it was unavoidable; after all, it was our common experience. The inevitable question, what camp were you in? Tule Lake? And the instant judgment, not stated, an occasional oh? in their eyes, look and manner would diminish me. Why was I diminished? Was it guilt? It shouldn't have but....

Later when I went to college in Los Angeles, I avoided other Japanese American students. In fact, I became something of an eccentric, wearing a hat on campus when nobody else did. Among Nisei, I was a loner, concentrating on being a student, the business at hand. Some white veterans, also serious students who wanted little or nothing to do with their experiences, became my friends. It was ironic—men who had fought in the war, even against the Japanese, were friends with someone who had been in Tule Lake, a camp infamous for holding the so-called "disloyals." We rarely talked about the war or the wartime. Occasionally, the subject came up and I would tell them that I had been in camp. They would say they had heard about it and shake their heads, but they never asked what camp I was in. If they did, they didn't know or care and I felt safe with them in their ignorance and indifference.

Asparagus Cutting

The other day I bought some asparagus, probably the first
ones to appear on the market this year, at sixty-five cents
per pound. On our limited budget such an extravagance
is almost a crime, and my wife didn't know what to make of it.

"Are you all right?" she finally asked.

"I'm fine," I said.

So we had the asparagus that night and we enjoyed them
immensely without once mentioning or even thinking about what
they had cost.

But I've always been soft on asparagus, ever since that summer I spent a hundred days at an asparagus camp. This was soon
after we had been released from camp, when my main concern
was to make money quickly. The lure of twenty dollars a day had
brought me to this primitive labor camp where I had to wait out
the rainy season, sleeping at night in the non-electric bunkhouse,
falling deeper and deeper into debt for the board, and wondering
when, if ever, the "grass" was going to sprout.

At first we were a team of eight but after the first race, we
lost four members. They left, vowing never, never to return, casting grave doubts in the minds of those of us left behind. It was a
race, for the asparagus do not really sprout until the weather gets
good and warm. When another fellow joined us we became a

permanent team of five, probably the perfect number for cutting asparagus as a team.

We were able to last the season and we each made one thousand dollars. This was after everything was accounted for—the board, the money we had taken to camp, the trips into Sacramento, meals there, movies, taxi fare back, equipment, even a gift for the cook-san.

I've forgotten the jargon and many of the details of the work. I remember there was a crew of German POW's, tall Nordic types in shorts, working the adjoining field. To finish a line took anywhere from half an hour to over an hour depending on the number of sprouts. The way we figured it was—when we had done a line and come back another, it was time to go and relieve ourselves.

I was always the last one. That probably meant that I was the slowest, but speed didn't count for everything. We were paid by the piece, the amount of asparagus we cut. But I was always grateful to the stronger members who helped the slower ones, making it a cooperative team effort.

I remember how good the coffee and doughnuts were at 9 a.m. in the field, how the food at meals tasted so good, how the hot tea was like medicine for my tired body. I remember also wanting to hear music of any kind, but those were pre-transistor days. Most of all I remember the backache, how at night I lay flat on my back, grim and unspeaking, mentally preparing myself to get up the next morning when the mess bell would ring at 4:30 a.m.

Thinking back now, I often wonder how I was able to do it. I heard later that many people had called me a fool for trying it. They were right, but I didn't have much choice at the time. It was extremely hard work; nothing I've done since compares to it. But having done it, I can appreciate physical labor. When I hear how hard our Issei parents worked, I have an idea how that must have been.

Ironically, what the asparagus cutting did for me was to set me free from such labors. With the thousand dollars I was able to go to college. During the first two years of school I worked nights as a porter at a Bullock's department store in downtown LA. It wasn't until my junior year at UCLA that I felt sufficiently removed from the asparagus experience that I could dip into my nest egg. I quit my part time job; I started to enjoy college and have some social life.

I don't think that I have ever worked with as much determination as I did that summer in the asparagus field. I remember the boss praising me not for my speed or skill but for my tenacity. Nowadays, operating on three or four cylinders, I sometimes have a vague feeling that I just might be cheating myself.

OUR WEDDING. SADAKO AND HIROSHI
KASHIWAGI, BERKELEY BUDDHIST TEMPLE
(BERKELEY, CA, AUGUST 31, 1957)

Our Wedding

I met Sadako, the love of my life, in Berkeley but I had seen her in Tule Lake when she was a young girl of 12. I was a Block Manager, sitting outside, smoking, and watching the girls go by. Sadako would come to our block everyday to visit her friend. She would flit across my sight and I noted her lively spirit and innate grace.

Twelve years later we would meet in Berkeley and fall in love. We were married on August 31, 1957.

It has been a good marriage—of two people who were right for each other. We think alike; we often have the same thoughts at the same time and the uncanniness always makes us laugh. We have great respect for each other and for all of life. We feel blessed and we are thankful.

Sadako has given me so much—her care, her support, and most of all her love. She has made my life whole and complete. She has been a wonderful mother to our three sons who are decent human beings, kind and thoughtful of others. My wife deserves the credit for their upbringing, especially when they were very young when I was so occupied earning a living.

I love my family—my wife, our three boys, and our daughter-in-law—they are very special to me—my pride and joy.

In tribute to the late Bishop Kanmo Imamura, who married us, I wrote the following:

I was wearing a tweed suit, a bit too warm for the season but newly purchased. Sadako had on a light gray cocktail dress, very appropriate for our wedding. It was cool in the chapel; Jane played the organ for us. Sadako's sister Tomiye and my friend Frank stood as witnesses. I suppose we were being selfish but we wanted a simple wedding, just for us. There were no guests; the Imamura children were our surrogate guests. I don't remember why our families weren't there. We probably didn't ask them to come, they were so busy and far away. The candles were lit on the altar; we stood in front of the image of Amida Buddha. Then Sensei in a white robe solemnized our marriage with a few well-chosen words and with a warm smile wished us well. We were humbled.

Through the years, through much happiness and some sorrow, we have often recalled that very private moment in our lives. I write of that long-ago scene now to say how honored we were by Sensei and how grateful we have been through the years for his quiet words of wisdom.

They say you are gone, Sensei.

We wave and wave.

Moving to the Freeway House

We were living in North Oakland, near Berkeley, but we couldn't live there any more. Our two boys were sleeping in the living room, and the overstuffed sofa was squeezed into the dining room where the heavy table, though pushed into the corner, took up half the room. Because we used the table as a desk, a sewing table, a television stand, a general catchall for magazines, books, bills, newspapers, letters, diapers, and as a dining table, it was a nuisance. We had to live around it, getting into each other's way. Yet the dining room was the only place where we could live half-normally, where we could talk and laugh occasionally, and where the children could drop things on the carpeted floor without the neighbor below pounding on the wall. We couldn't understand why he did this, why he didn't come out and tell us instead of pounding on the wall. It was so unnerving that we developed a habit of tiptoeing through the rest of the apartment, and when the children cried at night our first thought was to carry them out to the dining room, fearful that the pounding would start. After a while the pounding stopped, and we wondered whether it was because we were careful or because their own child began to crawl and bang on things. Still, somehow we couldn't trust a man who smiled and was so neighborly during the day, yet pounded on the wall at night.

So there we were, the four of us, living in the tiny room, crowded by a mohair sofa which we adored, a table which the landlord refused to remove, and a neighbor with whom we were getting more and more distant.

We began to scan the papers for apartment rentals and told our friends that we were thinking of moving, but whenever there was a lead we always found some excuse not to follow it. The thought of packing and unpacking; of borrowing or hiring a truck; of disconnecting the phone and getting a new one, a transaction in which I was certain we would lose money; of the kind of neighbors we might have; any one of these was enough to convince us that we were quite well off where we were. So, crowded as we were, months went by.

Then one day I decided to move. The decision was so suddenly and firmly set in my mind that my wife, taken somewhat by surprise, could do nothing about it. I had answered an ad for a flat for rent in San Francisco and had liked it immediately. I guess it was the rent most of all—ninety dollars for a six-room flat, unfurnished—I knew we couldn't do much better than that.

"You really want to move, don't you?" Sadako said, rather distantly, as though chasing a rapidly fading hope.

"Yes," I said, "don't you?"

"I'm not so sure."

"But why? We've been thinking of moving for months."

She had been halfway convinced that the flat was right when we went to see it, although she kept sniffing and shaking her head. It was she who noticed that the rooms had been freshly painted, a fact that had escaped me, though I was impressed with the cleanliness of the place. I was too busy mentally assigning rooms to the various members of the family. I must admit that I picked the room with the best exposure for my study and I looked forward to the day when I could be there by myself, away from the family—my wife and the kids. Going through the rooms, I located in my mind the few pieces of furniture that we owned and a few that we were thinking of buying. Sadako kept noticing how cold it was in the flat, and I reminded her that the heat wasn't on yet. We both agreed on the two back rooms, so sunny and bright. One was to be the playroom, and the other our bedroom. Through the window we could look down on a backyard, which wasn't much, overrun with weeds, but had possibilities, especially the swings for the children. In the distance we could actually see the trees on the hill and the sky. I liked the sky especially. The sight of the backsides of the houses wasn't very pretty but optimistically I knew I would learn to appreciate it—the relationship of the lines and shapes, and the play of light and shade.

Sadako was in the kitchen taking inventory, noticing the fairly-new stove, the custom sink, opening cabinets, pulling out drawers, and always sniffing and making faces. The pantry with plenty of shelves made up for the lack of storage space. The back porch with room for the automatic washer was good, and there was a tub that was essential for the suds-saver. The owner and his family of wife and four children, we learned, were our immediate neighbors in the middle flat below us.

"I'm frightened," my wife said, and she couldn't explain what it was that frightened her. Perhaps it was the strangeness of the city; perhaps it was the glamour of the city—the shops, the theaters, the restaurants, and the elegant peoples of the evening— that she had heard of or read about while growing up in a small town; perhaps it was the coldness of the city—the stories of loneliness and despair that frightened her. She has a strong sense of belonging. If now, living in the city, she is lost or frightened, she can renew this sense of belonging by visiting her hometown where the house in which she grew up still stands and where her family still lives. By filling herself with the familiar sights and smells, she can renew her longing for place.

As for myself, I don't remember a single house that I can consider home. There are many houses but I cannot picture in my mind one complete house, only fragments—a corner of a room where my bed stood; the front of a stove in a kitchen where I used to dress on cold mornings; a section of a porch where I used to play tag with the boys who stopped by on their way home from school; the top of the billboard where my brother and I used to sit with our legs dangling.

It seems that we were always moving; we didn't stay in one place for more than a year or two, but I remember one house where we lived for five years. Yet, that was the house that was torn down, forcing us to move. I remember it didn't take long for the men to tear it down, just a few hours while I was in school; when I went back during lunch hour the house was already gone and the men were clearing away the pile of weathered and rotted wood. It took a long time getting used to the fact that our house was no longer there, yet once removed from the mind, the house is difficult to restore.

The day we moved to San Francisco was a cold day in January. The heater wasn't working properly, and my wife could only think of how cold it was. We had tried to move systematically, yet it was almost impossible now to locate anything in the pile of things in the hallway. We tried to make the children's room as attractive and comfortable and inviting as possible. We put out the familiar toys—of course the teddy bear and the tommy cat—and I hung up the large collage that the older boy had helped me make. When it was up near his bed he said, "That's a good picture, daddy; we made it, didn't we?"

I was tired from going up and down the three flights of stairs, and was ready for a bath and bed, when Sadako suddenly exclaimed, "Mice!"

"There are no mice," I said.

Once we had the crib made up the baby went right to sleep as he always did and we said, "He's a good baby." But the older boy wouldn't go to sleep.

"Let's go home, daddy," he said. "Let's go home, mommy."

"Honey, this is our home now," my wife said.

"This is home," I said and my wife looked at me as if to say, "Is it?"

"It's cold," she said shivering and clutching her knitted

sweater. Then I lifted the boy, who was over three and too big to be carried, and sat down in the rocking chair.

"This is our home now," I said to the boy.

"No, this is not our home; this is freeway house."

I held him close and gently rocked him as I had done many a night when he wouldn't go to sleep as a baby. And he kept saying, "This is freeway house."

Early Parenting

Recently, I went to Kaiser to have my blood pressure checked and found the "No Blood Pressure Taken Today" sign. I started to complain and was told to call ahead before coming. To salvage the trip, I decided to walk to Haight Street past the neighborhood where we once lived.

Divisadero Street looked better than I remembered it; new buildings were up and old ones were in good repair. I was surprised that the sanding company where I once rented a floor sander was still operating. Scotty's Corner, where I had a hamburger on that first day I went to clean out the flat, was replaced by another business. I knew that the corner had been vacant for a long time. The funky grocery where we shopped occasionally was gone, but the busy automotive shop was still thriving.

Even on a cold morning, some people were outside visiting; it was still a Black neighborhood. Our building looked much the same; perhaps a bit rundown, the curtains over the windows looked ragged. We lived on the third floor flat. Our door was one on the far right.

My wife remembers only that it was unbearably cold when we moved in—January, 1963. There was no central heating, only two small heaters, one in the back room and the other in front. We lived mostly in the back where we had sunshine a good part of the day. There was always a draft and we kept plugging the holes under the front door and around the windows. It was over a year before we got over the peculiar smell of something rotting, decaying, probably dead mice or rats caught between the walls; it either dissipated or we finally got used to it

Our older boy Tosh called the flat "Freeway House," which was very apt as we were only a few blocks from Fell Street off the freeway. "No, this is Freeway House," he would say, longing for our former place in North Oakland. We were still making trips across the Bay to the children's shoe shop in Berkeley (they wore clunky corrective shoes that they hated) and to the pediatrician at Kaiser Oakland where the two boys were born. It was some time before Tosh would accept the new place as home.

But we enjoyed the space in the flat. Tosh could ride his tricycle down the long hallway and through the sparsely furnished rooms. We hardly used the front room; the room adjoining it was my study.

Many things happened that year—1963. Our third son was born late in October; it was early morning when I called for a taxi; my wife remembers that the driver seemed nervous as he sped to the Kaiser Hospital. Fortunately, we lived only a short distance away.

That Thanksgiving, my wife, still pale from her confinement, determinedly cooked and served a complete turkey dinner. Our guests were my supervisor, the Bishop Mr. Hanayama, his wife and their son. It was a quiet dinner, as we were still reeling from the shock of President Kennedy's assassination.

Working for the church headquarters, we barely got by on what I made. We didn't go anywhere; when we did, it was usually to a meeting in San Mateo when we went as a family. The kids would be asleep when we returned at night, and getting them up three flights I often vowed "never again." We would awaken the oldest and have him walk; I would carry the baby in my arm, football style, and the other boy on my back. If he hunched over, he would ride me lightly like a jockey without my holding him.

But there were also baskets of diapers, clean and soiled, tons of clothes, a stroller. My wife took care of some hauling but I had to make several trips up and down the stairs. Then I had to go park the car somewhere. It was a hard life.

My wife took the kids out daily—Hiroshi F. sitting in the stroller, Soji standing in the basket, and Tosh trotting along. Usually they went shopping at Safeway or Petrini; sometimes they went to the playground at Alamo Square. When our neighbors heard about that, they were appalled; they warned her to be careful, Alamo Square was a den of "sex deviants," they told her.

Then I stopped working and returned to school at UC Berkeley, another difficult year. An occasional translating job and a short stint at the Post Office as a temporary clerk were the only source of outside income that year. We lived on our small savings, some money borrowed from my brother-in-law, and a student loan from the government.

I don't know how we managed; sheer determination, I suppose. I was promised a job at the library as soon as I got my degree. My wife's training and experience as a home economics teacher were taxed to the limit. To her credit we never went hungry; even on our small budget we always had wholesome and tasteful meals and the baby had plenty of Gerber food, bought at special sales. In fact, my wife became an expert on specials and discount coupons. We had day-old bread and the kids wore recycled clothing.

We managed to keep up our Kaiser health plan; that was especially important with the kids. I remember spending many hours at the Kaiser waiting rooms. I learned to take a book along; in fact, I still do.

It was a year-long battle—commuting to Berkeley, driving around looking for parking space, walking to campus, attending classes, doing assignments, writing papers, taking exams. I remember having a sore neck the whole year. Bath time after dinner was sleepy time for me. If the boys now have an aversion to bathing I'm afraid I caused it. It was in—one, two, three; wash—one, two, three; out—one, two, three. I guess I took the fun out of bathing for them.

When I was finally graduated after a year and a half, my wife insisted that I participate in the graduation ceremony. Realizing that it was as much her achievement as mine, I agreed to attend, complete with cap and gown, photographs of me and the family, and a party given us by our friends.

The following Monday, I was working as a reference librarian in the Literature Department of the San Francisco Public Library, a full-fledged professional, earning a fairly decent salary for the first time in my life. I got my first paycheck after a month of work, during which I wore my one and only suit almost every day. Needless to say, the first check went for some clothes.

Soon after, we moved to the outer Sunset, near the beach and close to San Francisco State College where our children would attend the demonstration school. It was several years before we could pay off our debts and we could feel guiltless and comfortable eating out or going shopping or even taking a short vacation.

Sometimes I wonder about our experience. How did we do it? I guess we managed because we were young and full of energy and nothing was daunting. Why did we do it? We did it because we had to, because we were parents and the children needed our attention; because we remembered the care we received from our own parents. And it wasn't grim at all; the children brought us untold happiness.

It's many years now. The boys are grown and independent. My wife went back to Berkeley and got her master's degree and now she herself is a children's librarian. After twenty years I retired from my job at the library. As a member of the Screen Actors Guild, I wait for calls from my agent which are getting few and far between. I go to have my blood pressure checked and watch my cholesterol intake. What else do I do? Well, I shop and cook for the family on weekdays, clean house occasionally, walk two miles a day, and spend a little time in my room—a 4 x 7 semi-sound-proof cell, reading and writing—about the early years. There's some pleasure in that, too.

Our Neighborhood

I understand that we live in a "ferocious" neighborhood. Certainly, the people who visit us seem to have this impression. If they don't openly ask us whether we have any trouble, I know they're still wondering and maybe worrying for us. This is rather puzzling, since the idea never occurred to us. We moved here because we liked the six-room flat; it was old, but spacious, with plenty of light, and most crucial, the rent was within our limited means. We could tell that the neighborhood wasn't the cleanest or the most elegant in the city but that didn't deter us. We knew we would get used to it and after a year and a half we grew quite fond of both the flat and the neighborhood.

About the only complaint I have is against the dogs from other neighborhoods who visit us daily. I once knew a fellow who developed premature stoop shoulders by going around with his eyes fixed to the ground. When I asked him why he did that he replied, "You'd be surprised how much money I pick up this way." Well, my round shoulders are not from looking for lost coins but from dodging dog droppings.

Parking was quite a problem for a while. In fact, it became an obsession with our boy Tosh whose first words when I got home at night would be: "Where did you park, Daddy?" He would stand by the window for hours looking out for a parking space; occasionally when he found an opening (he could spot one a block away) he would run in to tell Daddy. The only trouble was I would still be at work. I solved the problem by parking where space was usually available, next to the Safeway lot some three blocks away from our place.

Once, however, when I found a spot across the street and parked there, some kids threw orange pulp on the windshield and I had to clean the sticky mess with soap and water. When they did the same to the rear window, I decided they should be taught a lesson and chased the ten of them down the block. My only intention was to give them a good scare that I think I did for they scattered in all directions. But I learned, rather painfully, how terribly out of shape I had become.

Another time, some kids called me a "Chinaman" and when I didn't turn around and play their game, I heard them call out "fat ass." Now the Chinaman bit, I have heard many times before. But the second epithet was jolting, to say the least, as I like to think I'm still quite trim and far from having a middle-aged spread. But who am I to say how I look from behind, especially to kids sitting idly on apartment steps?

These are minor annoyances in this cosmopolitan but predominantly black neighborhood. Certainly, there is no hostility. The people are friendly if not overly sociable. Given time, we may yet become neighborly, although that will take some doing, for who in the city is really neighborly? People can live in the same building for years with no more than a perfunctory "Hello" when they meet. That is characteristic of city living.

But what's "ferocious" about our neighborhood? I think it only seems that way to outsiders, to people who don't live here.

Richard Brautigan

I planted the seeds
in the garden
just like you said
in your book
up came poppies
and Shasta daisies
and marigolds
a riot of flowers
in my garden
when I was expecting
pot
you fooled me there
Richard Brautigan

A Librarian
Looks at
Snails

watching
snails
coupling
I wonder
if they read
books on
sexuality

Jap

*I work in a library where we see all kinds of
people. Well, there's this retired San Francisco
fireman. Irish, I believe. He plays golf, at least,
that's what he says. He comes in every week to
return and check out books. I suppose he reads,
mostly mysteries, probably for his wife. And he
likes to spend time chitchatting with the staff,
especially attractive females, we have some you
know. Well, the other day he was talking with
this woman about his car, how he always kept it
in good condition, always went to this one service station, been going there for years, do good
work, great place, great people. But last week I
went there and the place had been sold—to
some Japanese. Well, I didn't stay there long,
hell, I didn't want no Jap workin' on my car.*

I couldn't believe he said this. I was sitting right
there. Did I hear wrong? I checked with the
woman if indeed he had said Jap. The woman
nodded gravely. I wondered what to do. I knew I
couldn't change the old guy but I couldn't let it
pass. He was talking to another staff member,
this time a male. I went up to him, we were
about eye level, he seated, I standing, and I
pointed at him. Hey, that's a good technique,
using the finger, the index finger, not the middle.
And I said, did you say Jap a moment ago?

Whhh…Japanese.
No, JAP!
There was a moment, I kept my eyes on
him and he was squirming.
Well, if I did, I apologize.
Okay, I said, and walked away.
I know I didn't change the old fart
but I felt good doing what I did.

Sunday Monologue

I t was the Sunday I wasn't planning to go to church service. I find listening to the message from the pulpit rather tiresome, even if the person has on a priestly robe. It keeps me from reading the Sunday paper and I hate getting behind in my reading. I subscribe to *The New Yorker* and I try to read it from cover to cover. That's a lot of reading; *The New Yorker* stories are notoriously long; if I have a good book to read, then I know I'll get behind; *The New Yorker* keeps coming and coming. I'm glad I don't live in LA or New York where the papers are thick and take many hours to read. This is not to say that I'm a slow, plodding reader, I'm not. But reading is my favorite pastime.

It was the Saturday before the Sunday in question. My plan on Sunday was to read the paper in the morning, catch some of the Giants/Mets doubleheader and watch Tiger Woods make mincemeat of the golf pros at the Masters tournament. But on Saturday I got a call from a casting person for the TV show *Nash Bridges* to be an extra on Sunday. I had to be on the set promptly at 6:30 a.m.

I drove, not trusting the Muni on Sunday, and I was there by six, wearing my dress up outfit—one of two I own; the scene was to be in a very upscale restaurant. I know I have to update my clothes, because extras are expected to bring their own wardrobe.

It was cold downtown so early in the morning. There were the trucks, semis, vans, and the police—the usual on a film location; breakfast things were laid out but I had already eaten. While getting my voucher for costumes and hours worked (a very important procedure), I met Frank and Alice, old buddies from the extra circuit. My wife and I had worked with them on a French film starring Belmondo on Alcatraz a few years back. They are veterans now, having worked steadily in films, commercials, and print ads; they had been on the *Nash Bridges* show several times.

We walked up the hill to Broadway to Frankie's, a nightclub, which was our holding place. There were six or seven Asians among the extras; soon we Asians were driven to Grant Avenue where our first scene was shot. Stand-ins for the stars—Don Johnson and Cheech Marin—in the familiar yellow convertible came down the street, turned sharply on Grant Avenue and parked; then cronies Frank and I crossed the street, shook hands and went our separate way. Other extras or background people as we were called were pedestrians too. That was the scene that took about six or seven takes.

Back at Frankie's, most of us changed outfits and waited. Then we went down the hill to the Cypress Club, where we would spend the rest of the day as patrons of this posh restaurant. I thought the décor was gaudy, not very aesthetic; most impressive for me were all the wineglasses, glittering in the light.

The real Cheech had several scenes while we pretended to be enjoying our dinner. I was paired with a friendly, young and beautiful Asian woman. It was my luck, but it was just pretend for a TV show. The last scene that took the longest had Cheech acting the part of a smartass sommelier who spills wine on a guest, upsetting him.

We were served appetizers—mine was a weird concoction that looked like a columned building made with potatoes for columns and fried sole for the roof, and an outline of a lawn. For the sake of realism I kept taking tiny bites of the food which was barely cooked. When the woman playing the waitperson came to collect the dishes, she was shocked that I had eaten the prop. "I hope you won't get sick," she said ominously. I worried a bit but nothing untoward happened. Maybe I was saved by the grape juice (wine) I had sipped during the scenes.

Since the filming went past the lunch hour, they would have to pay us two penalties, my young companion (a knowledgeable extra) informed me. After a sumptuous lunch, we were told it was a "wrap" and we were through for the day. This announcement and the signing of the voucher were the best part of the day.

When I got home around four, sleepy and tired, I was cheered by the good news—the Giants' sweep of the doubleheader and Tiger Woods' phenomenal win at the Masters.

On Borrowed Time

I am indeed grateful that I have lived this long. When I was in high school, people thought I would not live past twenty. Here I am eighty and going strong. I guess I licked the TB or tuberculosis that was the bane of our family. Or was I just lucky? A look at my chest X-ray will reveal scar tissues, evidence of a mild case during my childhood.

Whenever I had a skin test (I used to dread it) the skin would bubble up, a positive reaction. They would order a chest X-ray and sure enough there would be the scar tissues. I wasn't so sick that I needed treatment; I was told to take it easy. Get lots of rest and drink milk. Milk was always medicine to me and I never liked it much; sometimes I took it with a vanilla wafer, which made it seem like eating ice cream; it is ironic that lately milk has lost some favor as a health food.

When I was a teenager, father had active TB but he would not go for treatment. People with TB were isolated in a sanatorium, and father, who was running a grocery store, felt that if he went away, mother and we children, who were still in school, would be hard-pressed to survive. So he sacrificed his health for us. Mother pleaded with him to get treatment but he was a stubborn man. I remember ugly arguments; both parents were frustrated and fearful that people would find out. Meanwhile, we were being exposed to TB, a highly contagious disease.

Mother tried hard to protect us and I feel that I owe her my life in more ways than one. Everything that father used for eating or drinking, she would sterilize in boiling water after each use and keep separate. Father would always cover his cough; this was crucial, as I learned recently that one could catch TB from the bacilli in the air. And he would collect the sputum which he later burned. We suffered each time he coughed. There was always tension in the air; sometimes father would be so frustrated that he became violent, smashing his dish or rice bowl. It was frightening.

One day I happened to be out in the back yard when I heard a noise in the garage. Odd, I thought. Who could be there? Then the engine of the panel truck suddenly ignited and the driverless truck hurtled past me at breakneck speed, stopping only when it banged into the bathhouse. I stood thunderstruck. I could have been standing in the way of the runaway vehicle. What was going on?

Then father came running out of the garage; he seemed flustered and astonished as I was. He quickly went to turn off the engine and check the truck and the bathhouse. The damage was minimal; the truck showed no ill effects and the dent in the tin wall of the bathhouse could be banged out easily.

"What happened, Papa?" I asked. He didn't respond. He had cranked the car to start it: why? I knew the engine always started with the ignition key. And why was it in reverse? These and other questions troubled me but father would not look at me; he seemed awkward and nervous, very unlike his usual confident self. I thought I had a glimpse of a dark, secret part of him. I was frightened—his eyes told me to keep it to myself.

Despite mother's precautionary measures, my little sister, Fusako, who was eleven years younger than I, died of TB meningitis when she was three and a half. My other sister developed TB many years later. She survived, however, thanks to the drugs discovered during the war, and was able to conquer it, though it took her many stays at the hospital.

After my junior year, father sent me off to Los Angeles where I finished high school. I wondered about this move. I took it as an adventure. Actually, though I was never told, it was to protect me; it probably saved my life. I regret not graduating with my original class; it is awkward when I go to the class reunions, but on the other hand I was able to survive. Living in Los Angeles also opened new vistas for me and made it easier when I started college there after the war. No longer a country bumpkin, I knew my way in the city.

One other thing that TB did was to stop me from becoming an athlete. When I was a sophomore in high school I was told "no PE and no sports." So there went my dreams of being an athlete. I'm glad my brother, who became an excellent football and baseball player, was able to give father, a baseball fanatic, a lot of pleasure. I often fantasize that I could have done that too; in fact, I think I had better instincts than my brother had, were it not for TB.

By the spring of 1941 father had abandoned the store and we were sharecropping. I was home working on the ranch when father hemorrhaged and we hospitalized him at Weimar Sanatorium. His TB was so advanced by then that there was no cure and bed rest was the only treatment. If only he had hemorrhaged earlier, he might have been shocked into going to the hospital.

Father did not go to camp with us, but remained at Weimar throughout the war; we did not see him again for over three years. In camp we were forced to make crucial decisions that affected the rest of our lives, and often the decisions were made out of fear, confusion and coercion. Though emotionally based, I think the decisions were honest ones that reflected our true feelings. I missed father's counsel, if only because he would have assumed the responsibility. However, as an upstart teenager I probably would have challenged him, even defied him. During the turmoil of the loyalty registration, father wrote us, suggesting indirectly that we make plans to leave camp. We rejected that idea outright. We were so intent not to register that we didn't even consider the difficult position father was in. When we told him our decision, he wrote back, "If that's how you feel, I won't say anymore."

Years later, I realized what suffering we must have caused him by remaining in Tule Lake, a camp for disloyals and incorrigibles. He was at the mercy of the white doctors and nurses who couldn't have been very sympathetic toward him, an enemy alien whose family was in a "disloyal" camp at Tule Lake. Though father never complained to us, I cannot imagine how it must have been. That's the greatest regret I have about our decision to stay at Tule Lake.

After we returned from camp, we visited father at Weimar as often as we could. Once he came out on a week's leave; I cherish the memory of that week, a rare happy moment I had with him as an adult. What was especially good was that my father and mother were together again, if only for a short time. Their life had been devastated and made lonely and difficult by that dreadful disease. Father died at Weimar in 1951.

Shungiku

Edible chrysanthemum
from the garden.
I bite it thoughtfully
and the mint taste
spins time and distance
until I'm face to face
with my Yamato origin.

Lost Football and Will

I spent a day at Drakes Bay one time. I was there with my friend Will. It was beautiful out there. I had taken my football along. We tossed it around. I couldn't pass very well, always kind of wobbly. But I could kick spirals, I told Will. He didn't believe me. He looked at me as if to say, "prove it." So I did—beautiful spirals that floated through the air, gaining distance and forcing Will to run back to catch the football. Then I kicked one that flew in the wrong direction—it landed way out in the water. I looked at Will. That's my football out there. Will just shrugged. It was too far out to go after it. We watched it—floating on the water, drifting farther and farther out to sea. That's my football. There was nothing we could do about it. Can you still see it, Will? I think so; yeah, there it is, way out there. Soon it was out of sight, only rising, now and then, a tiny dot in the distance. The football that had been so real in my hands was gone—irretrievably gone.

Much later now, the thought of the lost football and of Will, now gone, brings thoughts of other people and other days that have drifted into the distance at Drakes Bay.

Nostalgia Time in LA

Nostalgia is something we engage in more and more as we grow older. In excess it is not too healthy, I know, but recently when I was back in Los Angeles I let myself wallow in it.

"Nobody takes the bus in LA," my middle son Soji told me and indeed I saw few buses on the streets. He offered me the use of his car, but I didn't feel up to mastering the freeways. So the only alternative was to walk, which isn't strange to me—I walk four miles an hour. So I walked on Santa Monica Blvd, went shopping at Von's, and caught an early showing of *Raise the Red Lantern*, a wonderful film from China. I also walked to Westwood Village and wandered around; I followed the crowd into a Mongolian barbecue and had a great lunch of barbecued meat and vegetables in a bowl.

At UCLA I went into the student store looking for a towel with a Bruin insignia, to replace the one I had bought forty years ago when I was a student there (class of 1952). I had treasured the towel through the years, being careful not to use it, but now it was quite threadbare. When I approached a clerk, an Asian girl and asked about a towel, she looked at me as if I were a dinosaur and showed me a beach towel with a brown creature playing a ukulele and surfing at the same time. It was hip, I suppose, but hopelessly unaesthetic. I bought it anyway.

Walking back in my cheap tennis shoes, I must have done something to my left ankle. When I awoke the next morning, I couldn't stand on it, much less walk; Nuprin helped relieve the pain somewhat so that I could get around when I had to. Now I was really housebound; was this the life of a typical housewife? Pretty boring, I must admit.

I did some housecleaning but there was the whole rest-of-the-day, yawning before me. I spent a long time reading the *Los Angeles Times*. I read *China Boy* by Gus Lee, and I really enjoyed it, especially because it was set in the familiar Panhandle and Haight districts of San Francisco. And I read some of Woody Allen's biography. And I slept a lot. The painkiller I got at Kaiser made me sleepy; Soji had taken me there to have my ankle checked out.

One afternoon Soji took me around to some of my old haunts. First, we went to Dorsey High School, my alma mater, where I had been a student for one school year. It wasn't the best time to visit, as the school was in shock and mourning; a student/athlete had killed himself the previous day playing Russian roulette on the back of a bus. I heard this was the latest of several tragedies to hit the school. Police officers and school officials were milling about in the corridors. I assumed the students were in the classrooms. A kind Black woman arranged for us to look around. "It's pretty much the same," she said. Indeed the school hadn't changed, and the buildings were in good repair. I remembered the quads, or the unique arrangement of the buildings. The auditorium was now called Montgomery Auditorium, I assumed after Mr. Montgomery who had been the principal for many years. Everything looked clean and neat; I was impressed.

When I was a student there, it had been a new school; in fact, my class (Summer 1940) was the first graduating class to attend Dorsey all three years. The student body was mostly white, half-Jewish, about 50 Blacks, and 25 Nisei. Now the school was predominantly Black, both students and staff.

We went up to the library to look at my class yearbook. When the librarian brought out the book, I quickly turned to the page—there I was in a graduation cap, looking young and pristine. Later, I asked Soji what he thought of the photo and he said, "I was amazed how much you looked like me."

I remembered some of the teachers I had: Mr. Stone, my homeroom teacher who taught photography; Miss Merz from whom I had music appreciation; Mr. Hanson, the coach and gym teacher whose widow I had met in Sacramento and with whom I had reminisced about Dorsey; and Mrs. Moore, the drama teacher. I was the only non-white in her class; I remember trying out for the Shakespearean tournament, declaiming Antony's funeral oration on the auditorium stage. I tied for third or fourth and didn't make the team.

I used to walk to Dorsey from 39th and Dublin, where I was a houseboy in a doctor's home. It was a fair walk, about 30 minutes. A boy on a bicycle used to offer me a lift but after a couple of rides, I decided balancing on the handlebar was uncomfortable for me, difficult for him, and dangerous for both of us, especially crossing Crenshaw during the morning traffic.

We drove to the house where I had lived for nine months. We were standing in front of the English-style house but, painted white without trim, it looked different; only when I remembered it was next to the California-style house was I sure.

I could almost see myself in a starched white shirt and duck pants with two young boys in tow. Those boys must be close to sixty now; I looked for them in the phone directory, even tried calling some numbers. Wherever you are, you guys were great; you didn't give me much trouble; in fact, you often defended me against the bigotry of your playmates. When the other kids said "Jap"—as was common among kids then— you told them to stop, that it was wrong.

After the war we lived for two years in two adjoining hotel rooms on Towne Avenue near the produce market on 9th and San Pedro. Then we rented a house (a free standing whole house) on

Los Palos Street, off Olympic Blvd. That was in 1949. It was an unfurnished house but since we had no furniture, the kind white landlady who lived two houses away, furnished the house completely for us; the rent was an incredible fifty dollars a month. We lived there until I was graduated from UCLA in 1952.

Mother worked in a fish cannery on Terminal Island and came home on weekends, lugging fresh-caught fish. She stayed till Sunday evening, when she took the red car back to her hotel room in San Pedro. It was a good time; if there were any problems, it was the long bus commute to UCLA that took up so much time. To make time for study, I quit my part-time job as a night porter at Bullock's department store downtown. I had worked there for three years. My friend and I formed a theater group called "Nisei Experimental Group," for which I wrote my first play *The Plums Can Wait* in 1949.

We stopped at the house on Los Palos Street. While Soji and I were standing in front, a grey-haired man was peering out at us through the screen door, probably wondering why we were looking in. He came out to talk to us. He turned out to be a friendly man named Arturo, but he didn't think I had the right house. I didn't remember the house number but I was fairly sure that it was the house we had lived in; yet, there was something different about it; there was a tree in the front yard and a fence that hadn't been there. Arturo said he had planted the tree himself; the floor plan that I described to him was right and the garage in the back faced the alley and yes, there was a small apartment that adjoined the house where Marie had lived with her dog. This had to be the house, there was the freeway on the right and Olympic Blvd. on the left.

Taking Fourth Street to Li'l Tokyo, we passed Hollenbeck Park where I had played tennis on Sundays with some of my friends.

A flood of memories. What does it all mean? I asked Soji what he thought; it was not a fair question but he said, "Well, some things had changed and other things had stayed the same."

"He's right," I thought. The houses are the same, though they had been painted over many times. It was the things around them that had changed—the trees were older. What had been open fields around Dorsey High was now taken up with streets and houses, what had been theaters were now tabernacles and swap meet houses and the shopping malls along Crenshaw, where nothing had existed, already looked a bit depressed. And the people are gone, replaced by others.

"It's foolish to try to go back," was my next uneasy thought. I thanked Soji for taking me on this trip and turned to other thoughts. I was actually in Los Angeles to participate in a play that Soji had written: his first play. While driving to the airport, we talked again about the play reading, how successful it had been.

"I hope it's the start of big things for you, Soji."

"Yeah, thanks Dad," he said.

And I returned to San Francisco where I now live.

Paul

I wanted to see him again. That's why I decided to go to our high school class reunion—our first in 46 years. I hoped he would be there. Of my two hundred or so classmates, he was the one I wanted to see.

His parents were European immigrants who spoke English with a heavy accent. They owned a ranch and had Japanese tenants living and working on it. Our seventh grade class was divided into two sections: one made up of kids from the prominent white families and the other—the rest of us, mainly Japanese and poor whites. But I had history with the other group. When I stepped into their classroom, Paul would raise his hand and wave, volunteering to share his seat and textbook with me. When we were in the eighth grade, Paul came to our store to invite me to join their Boy Scout troop. He did this twice and both times I declined.

Through the years I have often wondered what prompted Paul to do that and how he felt about my casual response to his friendly gesture.

Surprisingly, the reunion was great fun and I'm glad I went. Of course it was awkward at first. It was impossible to recognize anyone, after 46 years. We kept looking at the nametags and I would notice the men's receding hairlines. Gone with the wind? After a while, after a drink or two, things were okay. We all looked like we did in high school. A former teacher—he must have been a hundred years old, but actually he was 92—gave a ringing oration (he didn't even use the microphone) just as he used to do in the auditorium before the whole student body. He made us feel like we were students again. And then there were prizes for those with the most grandchildren and children and triplets and twins. These are achievements? Bachelors got prizes too and those who had traveled the farthest. Someone from Alaska and another from New Jersey got the prizes. I kept looking around for Paul; there was no one who looked like him.

Then the master of ceremonies read off the names of the 27 deceased classmates; Paul was one of them. I left abruptly and quickly without a word to anyone.

But I wanted to know about Paul, what had happened to him. I took a chance and wrote to another classmate, asking about Paul. I hoped he would remember me and honor my request. He was a big time rancher and probably not used to writing personal letters, but within a week his reply came, telling me about the last time he had been with Paul.

During World War II, Paul was a fighter pilot with 50 successful missions over Europe. In December 1944 when he was home on leave, he and a few of his friends, who were also on furlough, spent an evening together. That was to be the last evening with Paul, who went back for a second tour of duty and was shot down and killed somewhere over France.

In 1944 I was in Tule Lake camp. I didn't know about Paul, all these years.

Ben

I went to Ben's memorial service yesterday. He had been cremated earlier. Although I hadn't known Ben much as an adult, he was a boyhood friend and a classmate. He was a few months short of his 75th birthday when he died.

In later years, I used to hear about Ben from our son Soji, who worked with him at the Kyoto Fish Market in San Francisco. Ben, it seems, took a liking to Soji. He told Soji that his grandmother, my mother, was a beautiful woman. When mother came up from Southern California on a visit, we took her to see Ben. He said she was still beautiful, just the way he remembered her; he said this despite her wrinkles and gray hair.

I played basketball with Ben in grammar school. Once we had a night game with the Roseville High School lightweight team at the high school gymnasium, about seven miles away. Ben drove his car and gave me a lift. I imagine he had a driver's license. I think he was driving since he was ten years old. We stopped for Joe, another team member, but Joe's father wouldn't let him come with us. Playing indoors in the gymnasium at night was a new experience for us but the size of the court was daunting; it seemed to take us forever to get from one end of the court to the other, dribbling or even passing. I don't remember much of the game, just that we showered after the game, drying off in the locker room with thick white towels. Ben got me home safely.

I also took kendo (Japanese fencing) with Ben.

When we were in the seventh grade, sometimes I sat with Ben in the same seat. I think we were sharing a textbook. Ben would fidget and look down at himself and when I tried to grab him, he would jump and the commotion would draw the teacher's attention and we would desperately try to look innocent.

Ben's early interest in cars carried over into his adult life—I learned at the service that he had worked for thirty years as a mechanic for a well-known garage in town. He had also been active as a Boy Scout leader.

Ben also liked popular songs and had quite a collection of 78's. Once he made a tape of love songs, by Frank Sinatra and Nat King Cole, and gave it to us on our anniversary.

Ben is one of eight Nikkei (Japanese American) classmates that I know who have passed on. I would sure like to see the others once again, before it's too late.

80th Birthday Celebration

What do you do on your 80th birthday? Something extraordinary of course, like climb a mountain, or run the marathon—like our youngest son Hiroshi F., who does both. Sadly, it's a bit late in the day for such heroics.

I always wanted to see my classmates from grade school and high school again. As my 80th year approached, I realized I better do something soon before it's too late. So early in the year I spread the word that I was inviting my Nikkei classmates to my birthday party in November. This was not only to convince my somewhat skeptical family but also to enbolden myself to actually carry out the plan.

Most of my surviving classmates live in Loomis or its environs where we grew up and went to school. We would have the party at our Loomis house, which would make it easy for people to come: hardly any driving. It almost seems like we bought the Loomis house just for this purpose. We bought it in 1989 as a safety net, since we have been renting our place in San Francisco. The original house was built in 1906 and rooms were added on as the need arose, without much thought to the design of the house. It's a funky old house but we love it. It has served as our " pied-a-terre." What's special is that it sits on a one half-acre lot, which to us city-dwellers seems like a huge estate. And we have fruit trees in the back. Thanks to Sadako's sister, Hisa, and her husband Sumito (since deceased), we have plentiful figs, peaches, plums, apricots, persimmons and apples in season. It is where we hold our annual New Year's Day breakfast for our family and extended family. What started as a simple breakfast of the traditional ozoni or soup with mochi or rice cakes and vegetables and sake to toast the New Year, has become quite an elaborate meal. But enough of this digression: back to the birthday party.

About a month before my birthday—November 8th—I sent out handwritten invitations to my classmates and wondered what their reactions would be. I later heard that they called each other when they received the letter. I could imagine their conversations: Did you get an invitation from Hiroshi? Yes, I did. I haven't seen him in ages, not since grammar school. I was about to call you when you called. I didn't know what to make of it. But wouldn't it be good to see our classmates again? I think it's a great idea. I'm going, are you? Well, I'll have to think about it, talk it over with my husband, it's so out of the blue.

I had set a response deadline for Election Day, November 5th, and the calls came to my sister-in-law Hisa who lives in Loomis. They were all coming. That's when I decided I would invite my high school classmates too. Many lived out of town and it was a bit late for written invitations so I called them. After the initial shock of hearing from me, they heard me out and agreed to come, even Harry who lives in Central California. He said he wouldn't miss it for anything; he would cancel all his other engagements (I knew he was a busy man) and come.

So the stage was set; the party would be on Saturday, November 9th, at 3 p.m. in Loomis. My wife Sadako and Hisa planned the menu. My brother-in-law Sumito would barbecue some chickens. We decided to substitute cha siu (barbecued pork) for sashimi (raw fish) when we learned that tuna was found to have excessive amounts of mercury and I didn't want to expose my friends to it even at this late date. Hisa would make the green salad and barazushi (sushi), her specialty. Sadako would make the potato salad, a little heavy on the starch, but who can resist potato salad? She would also prepare the kabocha (Japanese pumpkin) which grew in our back yard in San Francisco. Our son Soji from Pasadena offered to bring chow mein (store-bought of course); again heavy on the starch but what Asian can resist chow mein? My own contribution would be sabazushi (pressed sushi with mackerel), my specialty, and kimpira gobo (sautéed burdock), which is one of the things I eat to ward off gout. Our other son Hiroshi in Sacramento would make the fruit salad and pick up the cake. For drinks we decided on apple cider. "We 80-year-olds can't take anything stronger than water," I joked.

Our nephew Danny helped place two tables together to make a banquet table and we scrounged around for chairs—all the chairs in the house, two stored in the shed, a few borrowed from relatives, even a couple of odd chairs I brought from San Francisco.

Promptly, just before three, they all arrived. Even before coming inside, they were holding their reunion—hailing each other, shaking hands, and hugging each other. They were all so happy to see each other. That's when I knew my party would be a smash.

Everyone looked great; we all agreed that we had aged well. We were survivors; so many of our classmates had passed on. We could hardly believe we were 80 years old; we wished each other many more years.

After dinner, I asked Harry, who is famous for his fiery speeches on behalf of the farmers in Central California, to make a speech and he obliged and said how happy he was to have this rare opportunity to meet his old classmates and friends, to be back in Loomis, his hometown, where the air is pure and the values of friendship and love are still cherished. True to form, he was honest, eloquent and moving.

My daughter-in-law Keiko, a singer, offered us "Koko ni Sachi Ari" (Happiness is Here) in Japanese and English and "Moonlight Serenade," and her version of Louis Armstrong's "What a Wonderful World," for an encore, dedicating the songs to us octogenarians and we listened, remembering our youthful days.

My guests were Shiro Fujitani, Harry and Mary Kubo, George and Mitsie Makimoto, James and Betty Makimoto, Edward Shinkawa (since deceased), Marie Sugiyama, Jonathan and Karen Takagishi, and Roy (since deceased) and Grace Uyeda.

That is how we celebrated my 80th year, together.

HIROSHI KASHIWAGI HOLDING KABOCHA IN HIS BACKYARD.

Onsen Forever

*I*n Japan, at Hakone, I had my first onsen (mineral bath) experience. I passed up seeing the San Francisco Giants on TV for it. Watching the familiar Giants with Japanese commentary is like having spaghetti in Tokyo, familiar but different. But back to the onsen—once over the awkwardness of being nude in public, the onsen is an incredible experience, so relaxing. There are some rituals to follow: one should wash thoroughly before entering the pool; no one seems to shower standing up, either squatting or sitting on a low stool; a wash cloth, soap, shampoo, even a razor are provided.

Once in the pool, one should relax and enjoy the warm bath; I wondered about the use of the wash cloth as one does not wash in the pool; in fact, the cloth is placed on top of the head. I guessed that the cloth was for modesty's sake when one is out of the pool.

I came out of the bath, red and glowing, somewhat like experiencing a side effect after taking niacin that I do daily to control my cholesterol. While drying myself, I wondered where I should put the used towel. I looked up and saw a rather large sign with instructions; actually, I could read the Japanese though not so quickly; a gentleman seated nearby (I believe he was shaving) said, "You may put it over zare," sounding rather British. I thanked him and dropped the towel in the proper bin.

Now, they say that the natives can tell an American by the clothes he's wearing or how he wears them but I didn't have a stitch on. How could he tell? Maybe he noticed the tattoo on my behind, "Born in the U.S.A."

Meeting Relatives in Hiroshima

We had trouble again trying to find the right platform at Shin Osaka station. I could read the signs. but I guess I'm not a good follower of arrows. Anyway, by asking we managed to get to the right boarding zone for the train going to Hiroshima. People were generally quite helpful though sometimes they sent us off in the wrong direction; then confusion set in. That was the time I experienced some rudeness—I asked a clerk behind the ticket window if our tickets were for the non-smoking car and he pointed to the "kin en shitsu" on the ticket and told me it was non-smoking, his lips curling contemptuously. I should have known better; certainly I could have read that if I had been more careful; I guess I was being the dumb foreigner. Incidentally, that was the only instance of rudeness we encountered on this trip.

Once relaxed in our seats on the Shinkansen (Bullet Train), we bought two ekiben (box lunches). My anago fish lunch was a regional specialty. By pulling a string, some kind of steaming device was set off and I had a hot lunch in about five minutes. Sadako had chosen a Chinese lunch—an assortment of dim sum that looked good; she said it was delicious which surprised me, as normally she does not like dim sum. With tea our lunches cost roughly fifteen dollars.

Aunt Okada, Aunt Ishimaru (who we knew as Auntie Shimeno from our correspondence), Cousin Yoshimichi, and Second Cousin Shohei (who I mistook for a youthful taxi driver) met us. The ryokan (inn) where we stayed for two nights was near the train station. We had chosen it from a ryokan association listing. Apparently, it catered to foreign guests, many with backpacks. We would have preferred a few more amenities but it was an interesting experience. Auntie Shimeno did not approve of the place; she kept asking us how it was and we told her it was all right. The communal toilets and the wash troughs reminded me too much of the wartime camps. But with all the Caucasians staying there it was like being in America

Before going to dinner, we stopped at Auntie Shimeno's house where we were served tea and kashiwa-mochi, rice cakes filled with sweet bean paste and wrapped with kashiwa (oak) leaves, that Aunt Okada had made in my honor, my name being Kashiwagi or oak tree. The mochi was delicious; I had two in quick succession. We met Cousin Takeshi, the head of the household. His resemblance to Taku, Sadako's late brother, was uncanny. Taku and his family had visited them twice before his untimely death and Takeshi asked about his widow Helen and his two daughters Tamiko and Teruko.

Soon we were taken to the rather posh Terminal Hotel where we were honored guests at a fancy Kaiseki (formal) dinner. Though the guests were all family members, there were formal speeches by Takeshi and Auntie Shimeno who was actually responding for us, as I was totally unaware that I was supposed to respond. Next time I'll know better and I will be prepared. I know I disappointed a few people.

I sat next to the sculptor Katsuzo. Conversation was difficult in the formal setting. However, it picked up when Aunt Okada's grandson said that he was in a theater group that was doing Neil Simon's *Brighton Beach Memoirs* in Japanese. Then I related my theater activities and even Auntie Shimeno said she had a relative who was an actor; he had appeared as a priest in Kurosawa's *High and Low.* The kaiseki dinner was elegant and delicious and we appreciated the warm reception given us by the family.

Next morning we had an early breakfast of bananas, yokan (sweet bean confection) and tea, provided by the inn, and with our packet of Sanka we also had coffee and senbei (sweet crackers) Sadako had bought in Gobo which were so good I wouldn't mind going back for more.

We went on a rather long uphill walk along the river to Hijiyama Park. Along the way, we met any number of bicyclists; it seems they have the right of way and pedestrians are forced to make way for them or be bowled over. I noted that most of the bicycles were built low, I guess, to accommodate their short legs. Going past the Koyasan Temple, Sadako took a picture of me pointing at the character "ko" which was my name, having been named after the priest Kobo Daishi. On top of the hill was a huge, modern building—the Hiroshima Museum of Contemporary Art. The building was so wide that we could only photograph it in sections.

Then Cousin Yoshimichi, the artist who had lived in Spain, and Second Cousin Yoshimitsu took us to the Hiroshima Peace Memorial Park. We were walking along, admiring the trees and the shrubbery when we looked up and there it was—the atomic dome. We stopped in our tracks and gasped, looking at the skeleton of the dome and the ruined walls, an eerie, powerful testament to the devastating bomb. It was enough to set our minds back to August 6, 1945, the date of the bombing. The building had once been the Hiroshima Prefectural Industrial Promotion Hall.

The Atomic Cenotaph was another reminder. This monument, originally designed and built in concrete, had a special significance for the family as Cousin Katsuzo, the sculptor and an employee of the Iwasaki Marble Company, had carved it in stone. We also visited the sculpture of the young girl Sadako and her thousand paper cranes. My wife Sadako had a special affinity for this monument not only because of the same name but also because as a children's librarian she had told the story of the brave young girl, an atomic bomb victim, to many children in the library.

At the museum we had a tape-recorded commentary in English explaining the evidences of the havoc, pain, shock, suffering and death. It was unbearable. I felt sadness, anger, and shame that the people of Hiroshima had been subjected to this unspeakable horror.

That night, after a delicious dinner which Takeshi said was "tezukuri" or homemade, Auntie Shimeno related their experience during the atomic blast. Their house had been close to the epocenter. They had been downstairs—herself, Takeshi who was six and Katsuzo who was two—grinding soybeans, when the blast came. The second floor fell on them; they saw a red flash; they were saved because the roof had fallen on them; they were unhurt but trapped. Takeshi managed to crawl out and go for help. They were dug out. That first night they set up four poles and slept under mosquito netting. Her husband, an engineer, was out of the city working as a supervisor building Zero fighter planes. So he escaped the bomb. Then four or five days later they moved to the country so they escaped the radiation from the black rain that came a week after the blast. So far they have had no ill effects but Takeshi thought something might develop later in life.

Auntie said people hung effigies of Truman and threw rocks at them. Auntie said she saw people running around with their skin hanging down, crying for water. Many jumped in the river and drowned. They saw bodies floating in the river, red with blood. As an American I felt responsible. I should have said something but I didn't, couldn't. I just listened in horror.

Two statements Takeshi made that night will always remain with me. Pointing to himself, he said: "We are samurai (warriors)," and he said: "Consider it our pride," referring to the Atomic cenotaph carved by his brother. Then Takeshi's wife, who was living in the country away from the blast said: "The people who suffered the most during the war were the Japanese in

America who were put in camps." And I thought, "No, no, nothing imaginable could compare with what the people of Hiroshima went through."

Later in bed I thought of what had transpired earlier that evening and I was moved to tears. I had wanted to show Auntie Shimeno how I felt...what unspeakable horror they had known. But I felt trapped again—I was an American feeling responsible for it.

Sadako and I talked about it and decided our responsibility would be to tell others, as many as we can, those who can't come to Hiroshima and see for themselves, and bring them the message of the Hiroshima Memorial Park and its monuments: "Sleep in peace, the mistake will not be repeated."

Steveston: A Visit to a Fishing Village

I had always wanted to visit Steveston. I had heard stories about the town, how originally the folks had come from Mio-mura, a fishing village in Hidaka-gun, Wakayama-ken and how they spoke a rough dialect, unintelligible to outsiders. My parents were from Wakayama-ken, Hidaka-gun, though from a different, more inland village; my father had been a fisherman on Terminal Island.

The bus driver assured me that he would go to Steveston. So I sat back. The concierge at the hotel after some effort had given me good directions. We were heading south on Granville Street from downtown Vancouver. I had been afraid I would have to rent a car but here I was on a bus that would take me there in an hour. How fortunate.

Exactly at 8:30 a.m. the bus stopped at the end of the line and I got off. The Japanese owner of the Esso service station on the corner directed me to Moncton Street, just a block away. So I was finally in the fishing port of Steveston, SSW of Vancouver at the mouth of the Fraser River Delta.

Moncton Street with stores on both sides reminded me of the small town in Northern California where I grew up. Only the Net Shed Café was open. I hadn't had breakfast but I didn't feel like going in. I immediately recognized Hiro's Grocery from the book *Steveston Recollected* which I had read in the Vancouver Public

Library the day before.

Steveston was first settled in 1887 when a villager from Mio-mura named Gihei Kuno came to "America" or Canada and began salmon fishing on the Fraser River. He soon sent for other young men from his village. In time relatives, friends, and wives joined them. By 1910 there were 190 villagers and in 1926 there were as many as 1,057 persons including children who were born to the settlers.

Most of the businesses on Moncton Street seemed to be owned by Japanese: Hok-kai, sushi bar and restaurant; Puretic Fishing Gear, Inc.; Yo Commercial Fishing Tackle, Inc.; Momoi Net Co.; Koby's Billiards; Pacific Net & Twine, Ltd.; Nakashima Holding, Ltd.; River Radio & TV; Marine Garage; Nikka Overseas Agency, commercial fishing supplies.

I walked past the Steveston Hotel at the end of the block and out toward the pier where many boats were docked. A large fishing vessel was being loaded with cases of Pepsi Cola.

When I returned to Moncton Street, the shops were opening and I wondered how to make the first approach. Then I recognized the proprietor of Marine Grocery.

"I know you from the photograph in the book," I said.

"Oh? What book?"

"*Steveston Recollected.*"

"Yeah, I'm in that book all right," he said, pleased.

When I explained my interest and purpose and when I told him that my parents were from Hidaka-gun, he said, "Oh, I'm from Hidaka, too."

Though a native of Steveston, Mr. Morishita, the proprietor, was sent to Japan for his education and had returned.

"Oh, you're a Kibei," I said and realized my mistake. A Kibei is someone born in the United States who was sent to Japan for education and had returned. Mr. Morishita was a Canadian returnee. He said there were many people from Hidaka-gun but now there were also people from Shiga and Kagoshima prefectures. He has operated the grocery store for 32 years. When I asked if I could talk to a fisherman, he suggested Sakamoto-san.

"He should be at Marine Garage; he's there every morning," he said, pointing across the street. Sakamoto-san had already been there; I found him in a jewelry store. A tall, quiet-spoken man, Mr. Unosuke Sakamoto did not look his 79 years. He had been a fisherman since 1919.

"I arrived on February 16, 1919," he said.

Except for seven years during World War II when all Japanese Canadians were forcibly moved inland by the Canadian government and kept there, he had fished in the Steveston area for nearly half a century. He retired seven years ago.

For the first nine years he fished with his father who had come to Canada in 1900. After 1928 when his father returned to Japan, Mr. Sakamoto always worked alone from a small boat, netting and trolling salmon. He said he never experienced fear and didn't recall any close calls. In fact, he had saved others in distress.

Married in 1928, his family includes his wife, two sons, two daughters, seven grandchildren and one great grandchild. He spends his time coming to Steveston daily from nearby Richmond where he lives with his wife. His other time is spent working in his garden and traveling in the United States and Japan. He has been to Japan five or six times.

Sakamoto-san is not from Mio-mura but from nearby Hidaka-cho which is where my uncle lives. Mio-mura, he explained, was always impoverished. Because of the mountainous conditions and the rough shorelines, fishing was always difficult.

"That's why so many emigrated to Canada."

Later, the village became prosperous and famous as "America-mura" as the settlers sent back money and they themselves returned to live there with their savings.

"But most of the original settlers who returned are all gone," he said. Nowadays, Mr. Sakamoto and his wife are kept busy entertaining visitors at their home.

"Complete strangers write and ask to visit; sometimes they stay for a month," he said not uncordially. I thanked Mr. Sakamoto for the interview and he gave me his card.

I then stopped at the Steveston Post Office and Museum, a two-story wooden structure with a gabled roof and a board walk all to itself. On the upper floor museum there was an old photograph, ca 1897, of Steveston Japanese Hospital. The caption read: "Founded by the Japanese Fishermen's Association, 1895, for the care of the Japanese fishermen and their families; services available to all." The pictured staff included several Caucasian doctors and nurses and a single Japanese doctor.

I couldn't leave without going to Hiro's Grocery. Mr. Hiro Nuwatsukina, a native of Steveston, was cleaning the meat-slicing machine when I entered. A friendly man and a kendoist (Japanese fencing), he seemed well traveled in California—Los Angeles, Fresno, San Jose, Oakland, San Francisco. He kept mentioning names of people that sounded vaguely familiar. The shelves of imported Japanese goods reminded me of my father's store. Actually, the place was noted for its building that was designed by a Japanese architect and built before the war. No one seemed to know how old it was, but someone remembered that it was built in the year his daughter was born, and she was now 45. That didn't seem old for a building regarded as a city monument. It had a definite Japanese façade. The store was a hangout for retired fishermen and soon Hiro was hailing a couple of them.

"They're from Hidaka," he said by way of introduction. One was Mr. S. Uyeyama, a retired ship's carpenter, who had come to Steveston at age 16 in 1926. He was from Nada-cho in Wakayama-ken. The other was Mr. Itsuji Hamade from Hidaka-cho. He was born in Steveston, sent to Japan at age seven and returned when he was 17. He had been a fisherman until he retired four years ago. Though bilingual, both spoke to me in Japanese—not rough fisherman dialect but proper standard Japanese. But their accent and intonations were definitely Wakayama. Listening to them, I could hear my father speaking when he was alive and my mother when she was younger before her accent was corrupted by broken English and the dialects of other prefectures. I explained that I had to catch a bus back to Vancouver.

"Ogenkide—be of good health," we said, as we shook hands and parted.

A Meeting at Tule Lake

Most of this poem was written on the bus en route to the second Tule Lake Pilgrimage, in April 1975. The attendees were mainly young college students.

The bus ride to Tule Lake
in the night over dark highways
rain through the flatlands
and snow beyond Weed
up, up to the roof of California
was a movement back in time
back to the years 1943, 44 and 45
when I was 19, 20 and 21.
Being among you
sensing your youthfulness
hearing your strong voices
I search for reasons why
I came after 30 some years.
Tule Lake, Tule Lake—that
was a name I dared not mention
spoken warily, always with
hesitation, never voluntarily.

But you have made it
a common name again
of a small sleepy town
that it was
before we came here
before we were confined here
before it became Tule Lake
Relocation Center
before it became Tule Lake
Segregation Center
for disloyal Japanese Americans.
Yes, it's right that we're here
to see first hand where
18,000 of us lived
for three years or more
to see again
the barbed-wire fence
the guard towers, the MPs
the machine guns, bayonets
and tanks, the barracks
the mess halls, the shower rooms
and latrines.
Yes, it's right to feel
the bitter cold
of the severe winters
the warmth of the pot-bellied

stoves and the dust storms
how can we forget
the sand biting into our skin
filling our eyes and nose and mouth
and ears, graying our hair
in an instant.
Yes, it's right to recall
the directives
of the War Relocation Authority
their threats and lies
the meetings, the strikes
the resistance, arrests
stockades, violence, attacks
murder, derangement
pain, grief, separation
departure, informers
recriminations, disagreements
loyalty, disloyalty
yes yes, no no, no yes
Issei, Nisei, Kibei.
These are words now
but they were lived here.
There were deaths and births
and lovemaking in the firebreak
with the warden's flashlight
shining on you.

Yes, and movies, socials,
dances, sports, card games
and religion.
Sewing classes, flower
arrangement, doll making
wood carving
beauty behind barbed wires.
Recreation was big
it was encouraged.
"Keep 'em busy
keep 'em occupied
keep 'em sane,
for heaven's sake!"
But a Chronicle reporter
observed: "There are
18,000 mental patients living
in confinement at Tule Lake."
So it is right that I remember
and tell it.
I wish I could share
the feeling I have now
with the Issei and Nisei
they who lived here
they who do not speak of it
who pass it off
as a good time experience.

Whatever we did here
the commitments we made
loyal or disloyal
compliance or resistance
yes or no
it was right!
Because the young people
make it so
because they seek the history
from those of us who lived it.
So we must remember
and tell it
we must acknowledge it
and tell it.
So we are here
the Abalone Mountain
the Castle Rock
the dry lake bed
where tules still grow.
But the barracks
where are the barracks?
And where Apt. 40 05 D?
Home once long ago
sold? demolished? gone.
Little remains
except what's trapped

in our heads
far back somewhere.
I'm glad I made this trip.
Somehow I feel
a meeting of youths
your youth, your energy
your enthusiasm, your
sense of justice
with the youth that I was
idealistic, intense, angry.
It's a happy meeting
it is even better
that I can stand aside
after 30 odd years
and see it, this meeting
to meet, to share, to learn
to struggle, to continue.
I sense an immense feeling
of continuity
with
you – all of you.
Yes. It's right, it's right
and I'm glad I came
back to Tule Lake
with you.

(Written and read at
Tule Lake, April 19, 1975)

Testimony for Redress

(Testimony given before the nine-member Commission on Wartime Relocation and Internment of Civilians, San Francisco, 1981)

Mr. Chairman and honorable members of the Commission on Wartime Relocation and Internment of Civilians: My name is Hiroshi Kashiwagi. I am a writer, actor and librarian. I was living in Penryn, California when we were removed to Arboga Assembly Center. I was 19 at the time, two years out of high school, waiting for my younger brother to graduate so that I could resume my education. My father, who had tuberculosis, was confined in a sanatorium; he never went to camp and our only contact with him during the four years we were in camp was through correspondence. I want to emphasize that I was an idealistic, loyal American youth, ready and willing to serve my country when called upon.

I will confine my testimony to the loyalty registration at Tule Lake. Despite the threats from the administration and the pressures within the camp, I resisted the order to register and as a consequence I was declared "disloyal" and incarcerated at Tule Lake Segregation Center, a maximum-security prison, for the duration of the war. But I want to go back to the threats. We were warned that the refusal to register was a violation of the Espionage Act and we would face 20 years in prison, a $10,000 fine, or both. At that time the Project Director, accompanied by Army officers, appeared at key mess halls during lunch to read off the names of draft-age men expected to register. On February 21, 1943, 35 young men in a neighboring block were taken to Alturas County Jail at the point of bayonets. They were apprehended by an army of soldiers equipped with machine guns, tear gas bombs and fixed bayonets. I was a witness to the tearful scenes of family members parting with their sons and brothers; I was a witness to the capture of American citizens by American soldiers knowing that my turn was next and my suitcase was packed and ready.

The resistance to the registration broke down but not without tragic consequences. In our frustration and anger we turned against each other and the moderates who urged compliance and who answered "yes" to the questions were treated unjustly and even inhumanely by some. But can you imagine the confusion and the turmoil? What to do? We had no recourse to counsel. I held out to the end and never registered and was placed in the category of "disloyals" and detained at Tule Lake. Even then I had a good knowledge of the Japanese language and I could have served my country honorably and well as a linguist but such thoughts never entered my mind.

I won't review the conditions that prevailed in Tule Lake Segregation Center except to say that it was a psychologically abnormal, unhealthy place.

When the war ended we were the last to be released; as we returned "home" we tried to slip back as unobtrusively as possible. Whenever I was asked where I had been during the war, I always felt put on the spot. Sometimes I lied and said I had been back east, trying to hide the fact that I had been at Tule Lake. I always tried to block out that part of my life.

But after 35 years can you imagine my chagrin, my dismay, my frustration and my anger when I learned the real truth of the registration; when I learned that the War Department had determined that the registration and the answering of the loyalty questionnaire by draft-age Nisei were not compulsory; that the threats

PRESIDENTIAL COMMISSION ON WARTIME RELOCATION AND INTERNMENT OF CIVILIANS (NINE-MEMBER GROUP). HIROSHI KASHIWAGI, SECOND FROM LEFT, BELOW. (GOLDEN GATE UNIVERSITY, SAN FRANCISCO HEARINGS, 1981. PHOTO BY ISAGO ISAO TANAKA.)

of severe penalties had been a mistake and unwarranted. These facts were never revealed to us, never. We had been fooled. And I had been detained without cause and unjustly treated as an outcast. Once again I had been betrayed by my own government. All those years—thinking I had done wrong.

At least I'm thankful for this opportunity to unburden myself. Fortunately, I have some time left in my life; I'm going to live it as an American, as a free American, free of my shadowy past. To be an American is a privilege I appreciate; but to have been deprived by my own country.

Members of the Commission, if you represent America, then take this burden of guilt. It's no longer mine.

As for restitution, I will not accept rhetoric; only legal, tangible, monetary payment will be a meaningful apology.

Finally, I say to you, unburden yourself America.

Wayne M. Collins

He came at the lowest point in my life when I had just awakened from my stupor and realized I had made a terrible mistake. As a renunciant, I was now regarded as a "Native American Alien." What a preposterous predicament. I was a victim of the government's manipulation, of the hysteria within the camp, of the confusion in our family and of my own stupid inertia. What was to become of me now? The Justice Department had announced that all renunciants would be deported to Japan on or after November 15, 1945. What to do?

I first met Mr. Wayne Collins in late July 1945 when he was at Tule Lake to close down the stockade. I had not seen many Caucasians at close range in over three years, and I could not believe that this very Caucasian man, a refined, intense civil rights attorney from San Francisco, smoking incessantly, was actually on our side, outraged at our miserable situation. I joined others in seeking his counsel and he prepared for us a sample letter to the Attorney General requesting cancellation of the renunciation.

I was active in organizing the "Tule Lake Defense Committee" to work with Mr. Collins who agreed to be our attorney; no other attorney would take our case. The only group that assisted him was the Northern California branch of the ACLU and its director Ernest Besig who defied the national office of the ACLU and supported Mr. Collins.

I didn't realize how close we were to being deported to Japan until I learned about it later; only a few days before the Justice Department's order for repatriation was to take effect, Mr. Collins filed in the U. S. District Court in San Francisco mass proceedings in habeas corpus to stop the repatriation. A last-minute stay issued by the court stopped the deportation of the renunciants, many who were already on board the ship to Japan and were literally pulled off by the attorney.

Mr. Collins also filed a mass suit to void the renunciation and to restore to each of us our U. S. citizenship.

We requested a hearing to present our case—the circumstances and the cause of our renunciation and our desire to remain in the United States. The hearings were held in January 1946 and, as a result, all those who had requested a hearing were released in early March 1946, my brother, sister and I among them.

Good news came on April 29, 1948 when District Judge Louis G. Goodman issued a judgment canceling all renunciations. A year later, his final judgment declared that the renunciations had been unconstitutional and void, and he restored citizenship to over 5,000 of us who had renounced.

However, the government appealed and on March 1,1950 the Ninth Circuit Court of Appeals, based on the testimonies of some JACL (Japanese American Citizens League) members, threw out Judge Goodman's mass judgment. One good thing that came out of this decision was that my brother and sister had their citizenship restored as both had been under twenty-one at the time of renunciation were judged legally incapable of renouncing their citizenship.

A petition to the U. S. Supreme Court for a rehearing made by Mr. Collins was rejected. There followed months of tedious and time-consuming tasks, of entering individual suits for each of the 5,000 clients. Before the case was completely closed in 1968, Mr. Collins and his staff had prepared and filed over 10,000 affidavits.

A set of questions prepared by Mr. Collins, was mailed by his secretary Mrs. Chiyo Wada to each of the clients and the responses, often handwritten, were turned over to the attorney. Many Kibei responded in Japanese and Mrs. Wada translated them for Mr. Collins. A corps of young Nisei women worked in turn often till late at night typing the affidavits. It took over six months to complete and file the affidavits for the 5,000 clients.

Years passed while our status remained in limbo. I graduated from UCLA with a BA degree in Oriental Languages, couldn't find a suitable job, came up to Berkeley, enrolled as a graduate student, studied art history, participated in campus theater, and did part time work to sustain myself. In 1957 I was hired by the Buddhist Churches of America headquarters as English language secretary and editor. This was my first full-time job that made possible my marriage in August of the same year.

It was on May 20, 1959, amid much fanfare and publicity, that the Attorney General William P. Rogers finally restored our citizenship and 4,978 Nisei were again United States citizens. The Attorney General also publicly admitted the mistake made by our government. Though the Attorney General and the Justice Department were lauded for their "magnanimous" act, the true hero and champion of democracy was Mr. Wayne M. Collins. On March 6, 1968, twenty-three years after he had stopped our deportation, he announced the end of the renunciation proceedings.

Below is the affidavit that Mr. Collins wrote and filed for me.

"I did not want to apply for repatriation to Japan. I delayed doing it as long as possible. My mother, Kofusa Kashiwagi, brother Ryo, sister Eiko and I didn't want to go to Japan and had no intention of going there and leaving my father, Fukumatsu Kashiwagi, who was suffering from pulmonary tuberculosis and was a patient confined to the Weimar Sanatorium in Weimar, California, where he later died in 1951.

"I was employed at Tule Lake as secretary to the Block Manager in Block 40. The first Block Manager was Mr. Sumitomo who later went to Japan and next was Mr. Handa.

"When people were brought to the Tule Lake Center from the

W.R.A. camps to be segregated and sent to Japan, my mother, brother, sister, and I were afraid we would be sent away from California where my father was in the sanatorium and we would finally have to face relocation in a distant State where we would not be able to make a living and would encounter racial discrimination like we had been hearing happened to so many Japanese Americans and their alien parents. Many of the people who were brought in from the other camps talked and told us that all the aliens in Tule Lake would be separated from their children and be deported to Japan and that citizen children better request repatriation to prevent separation from their parents and to avoid getting in trouble when the families got to Japan. They emphasized that if the citizen children didn't sign up for repatriation they would have to face staying alone in camp until they were relocated in distant States where their security would be threatened. These things kept us worried. As secretary to the Block Manager in Block 40 many people came to me asking for help in filling out the repatriation forms because they feared separation from their families and relocation. Learning their reasons only confirmed the like fears my mother, brother and I had. My mother became so alarmed she repeatedly insisted that we apply for repatriation. I delayed. There was much agitation in the Block for repatriation and it broke out into open hostilities in our Block. Groups of people questioned everyone about how they stood on the subject. One day when an Issei spokesman for a group of the segregatees came into the office and asked for a list of those who requested repatriation and I refused to give it to him I realized that I had to send in an application for my own safety as people who refused to apply were being called 'White Japs' and 'Inu' and a number had been beaten up by unidentified gangsters.

"I resented the questioning of my loyalty. Earlier I had applied for student relocation to the WRA officer in the branch relocation office in the camp. He said it was futile for me to apply for student relocation because I didn't have enough money to be able to pay my living and tuition expenses. This was a big disappointment for me. I was 20 years old then, my father was in the sanatorium and the future looked very dark for me and my family. I registered for the draft in Tule Lake in 1942 and was given 4C enemy alien classification because I was of the Japanese race. This hurt me. When the Questionnaire was to be answered we were worried. My mother pleaded with us not to answer because she was afraid if we answered Yes to questions 27 and 28 that there was a likelihood that we children would be relocated and that I might be drafted into the army and that she would be kept in camp and ultimately be sent to Japan and be separated from us and my father. When I was called for my interview I said I objected to the questionnaire because it was unfair to ask it only of American-Japanese and not of American-Germans and American-Italians. But because there had been the threat by notice and rumors that anyone who did not answer the questionnaire would be sent to jail we were worried and didn't know what was the right thing to do. Under these worries I gave No answers to questions 27 and 28. I told the official that I did not want to answer the questionnaire while I was held in camp and treated like a dangerous alien but he said I had to answer those questions one way or another and so I gave No answers as a protest because the Government was treating me like a disloyal alien.

"Mr. Yoshida, one of the Issei leaders of the Hoshi Dan in Block 40 told me that for my own sake I must renounce citizenship and should send a letter notifying the Attorney General. He tried to get me to join the Hoshi Dan. I refused. Mr. Mori, Mr. Kimura, and others of their group kept telling people they better renounce citizenship and they would cite examples of people who didn't and who got attacked. Their organization was conducting marching demonstrations around the camp when I was told those things and the atmosphere of the camp was menacing. I was afraid it was too dangerous to try to be different from the rest of the people and find myself a marked man. We were afraid to speak in English because we would be considered as White Japs. My mother pleaded with us to send for the forms because we were fearful something would happen to us if we didn't. There was no protection for us against these dangers. The police were not able to protect us. The wardens were just fire watchers. We couldn't talk intelligently without someone threatening another. There were stealings, beatings and killings. Having refused to join any of the organizations and not having sent for the renunciation forms, I realized I was a marked man if I didn't do it. I realized the fears that likewise compelled so many of the people to make such applications for whom I filled out the forms that I was afraid of what would happen to me if I didn't do it also.

"At the hearing I was afraid. All I wanted was to get through with it. I could hardly speak. We knew the questions that were to be asked from previous interviews. I had not talked with a Caucasian in over three years and because of what had happened to us I had a feeling of fear, distrust and resentment.

"There were reports that the other camps were being emptied by people relocating and that Tule Lake would be closed and we would be sent outside and then there was a report Tule Lake would be kept open for a while. My mother was in fear of us having to relocate because we had no place to go home to in California and she was afraid to go elsewhere. I wanted to try for relocation but didn't dare leave my mother alone in camp. She believed if we children had renunciation hearings we could stay in camp with her and would be safe from the dangers outside. We were all afraid too that if we didn't have the hearings that something would happen to us from the Hoshi Dan organization. Members of the Seinen Dan and the Hoshi Dan were taken away from Tule Lake just before my renunciation hearing but there were lots of their crowd in camp when I was called for my hearing and it was not safe to go against what the crowd was doing.

"Living through all this terror with mixed worries and fears I was not convinced of the significance of renunciation except that it relieved me of the worst of my tensions and fears and I felt that I was no longer in danger of separation, relocation and physical harm.

"On Sept. 5, 1945, I wrote a letter to Hon. Edward J. Ennis requesting cancellation of my renunciation. On Sept. 28, 1945, I wrote a similar letter to Hon. Tom C. Clark. The delay was due to ignorance. I thought there was nothing I could do about it. I was also afraid to act individually. I was not convinced of the gravity until told by Mr. Wayne M. Collins. I did not even trust him at first because he was a Caucasian. I could not believe that a Caucasian would be concerned about us. When I was sure that he was sincere I took his advice.

"There are many factors for my actions. First I was very young and idealistic and easily hurt. Before the war, I had come to identify myself more and more as an American. Once I remember my father tearing America apart and I was trying to defend America. When my father had almost convinced me that he was right, I cried, 'But I'm an American, Papa.' And I said this with tears in my eyes.

"I was bitter about evacuation and my refusal to answer the loyalty question was a protest. If my father had been there I think it would have been different. We would have talked it over. But my mother was only thinking of our momentary security. Yet I was always bothered by the fact that I was considered disloyal. I would have been much happier if I could have signed 'Yes.' I think that this feeling of guilt was the root of my later actions. I believed that I was not wanted in America, that I was a criminal. I didn't know where I would go or what I would do. I didn't think beyond the present day. I lived in fear. There was no law or justice. The only way to settle things eventually was by threats or beatings (often at night). There was also the sentry. Once a military police rapped on our door and asked if we knew of the man he had caught after curfew. Arrests like this and the shooting of the Okamoto boy made me believe all Caucasians hated us and I distrusted them and I was afraid of them, too. I did not want to repatriate or renounce my citizenship. I did it only to be safe, to feel safe. Even while going through the procedures I didn't realize the significance of it all. I had no intention of going to Japan and leaving my sick father behind."

In December of 1971 when I was working as the Branch Manager of the Western Addition Branch of the San Francisco Public Library system, I sent Mr. Collins a Christmas card with a note thanking him for all he did for me in restoring me as an American, making possible the life I enjoyed now. He sent me a letter in response that reveals so much of the character of this great man who as the agent of democracy worked hard and long to right the wrong that we had suffered. I value this letter more than anything I have, more than the letter of apology signed by President George H. W. Bush and the reparation check for $20,000 that I received from the government in 1988. I am one of thousands who owe Mr. Collins a personal thank you.

In addition to our renunciation case, Mr. Collins supported the Yasui, Hirabayashi, and Endo cases, rescued hundreds of Peruvian Japanese from being removed to Japan, took the Korematsu case to the Supreme Court to challenge the constitutionality of the evacuation and internment, and spent over 25 years in defense of Iva Toguri d'Aquino, who was falsely accused of being "Tokyo Rose," to vindicate her good name and restore her U. S. citizenship. Upon his death in 1974, his son, also Wayne M. Collins, continued as Iva Toguri's attorney and was successful in securing for her on January 19, 1977 a presidential pardon from President Gerald R. Ford and the restoration of her U. S. citizenship.

Though motivated by his fierce devotion to the principles of fair play and justice, the elder Mr. Collins was often reviled as a "Jap-lover" for his work defending Japanese Americans. Yet, it seems he had a special affinity towards Japanese Americans. Mrs. Wada cites her family's long-standing friendship with him—at first with her father Mr. Senri Nao and with her and the Wada family. It began one day in 1917 when Mr. Collins, an eighteen-year-old sailor, appeared at Mr. Nao's art and gift shop on Grant Avenue in San Francisco and continued through the years until Mr. Collins' tragic death in 1974.

WAYNE M. COLLINS
ATTORNEY AT LAW
MILLS TOWER, 220 BUSH STREET
SAN FRANCISCO, CALIFORNIA 94104
421-5827

December 29, 1971

Dear Hiroshi Kashiwagi:

Your thoughtful Christmas card carried a touching
message. Surely you are too charitable in your thoughts
of me.

Our government deliberately perpetrated an outrage
on our citizens and aliens of Japanese ancestry without
justification. Neither it nor its servants appear to be
repentent for the evil evacuation and consequent loss of
liberty and property it caused to so many thousands of our
people and the injuries it inflicted on them. All of its
victims were innocent of any wrong doing whatsoever. None
of them posed a threat or any danger of any nature to our
security. On the contrary the victims were the most law
abiding and patriotic members of this nation.

Those whom the government forced to renunciation of
citizenship which was unconstitutional and void for duress
were the only ones who tried to fight back against the grave
injustices inflicted on them for this was the only avenue
open to them to reveal their opposition to injustice.

I neither deserve thanks nor seek credit for the little
I was able to do to right the wrongs done to you and the many
thousands of others who likewise were unjustly treated and
absued by our government. The little I did was done, I truly
believe, simply as an instrument-for what was accomplished
was purely providential.

It was a pleasure to receive your Christmas card in
remembrance of things past and I was delighted to learn that
you are the Librarian in Charge of an important Branch of our
Library.

You have my best of wishes for your continued success,
and for long, useful and happy lives for you and all the
members of your good family.

Sincerely,

Wayne M. Collins

LETTER FROM WAYNE M. COLLINS TO HIROSHI KASHIWAGI.

Reading, Writing, and Acting

R eading, writing and acting have been an integral part of
my life since childhood. They sort of dovetail each other.
It all started in Japanese since I didn't speak English
until I was about seven in the second grade at grammar school.

Every Friday night my father would help me prepare my
Japanese language lesson, reading the text while I looked on. He
read it twice— the first time in a somewhat leisurely fashion as
the material was new to him, the second time a bit faster —and
that was it, there was no third time. I was expected to know my
lesson by then. So I learned to concentrate totally while he was
reading and when I was called on to read the next day, I rattled off
without so much as referring to the text. That was my early training, not only in reading but also in acting, since I developed the
ability to memorize quickly and visualize the words. This served
me well later when I had to take tests in high school and college;
I could visualize exactly where on the page the answers to the
questions were. All I had to do was to mentally lift the answer
from the page and transpose it onto the test paper. That was
happy test-taking.

I suppose I have a "photographic memory." When I was acting
and had to learn lines I would picture exactly where on the page
the lines appeared. But if the script was rewritten or changed as

often happened, then I would have to not only relearn the lines but reimagine them in their new location. Of course, learning lines is a basic and mechanical process; acting begins only after the lines are learned.

As for reading, I think I got the habit of reading from my parents, who were inveterate readers. Father would buy their monthly magazines at his favorite drug store in Sacramento. Father's magazine was *King*, geared for the male reader, and mother's was *Shufu no Tomo* (Woman's Companion). Although they were faithful to their own magazine, after finishing their respective magazines, they exchanged them. It meant more reading material though, requiring a new mindset, but I suppose fiction is fiction, no matter what the gender of the reader. Of course, there were other materials besides fiction. I didn't read the magazines myself; I thought they were for adults. I might have flipped through them looking at pictures and ads, but once, after seeing a movie based on a novel by Kume Masao which was serialized in one of the magazines, I read it and really enjoyed it. I was around ten years old reading adult fiction in Japanese. Though I couldn't read every word, I could follow the story because I had seen the movie. I realized then that reading was just as pleasurable as seeing a movie or even better as it was more detailed.

I was a sports fanatic as a child and have been throughout my life. I'm embarrassed to admit that every morning I read the sports section of the newspaper before I read anything else. The world could be coming to an end or the president could be involved in a sex scandal, still I would reach for the sports section. I know I got this mania for sports from my father who was a baseball fanatic. Though he could carry on a simple conversation in his broken English with a Caucasian, he could not read English. Once he had enrolled in an English class taught by a Christian missionary but he left after one lesson because he didn't like the religious references. So he depended on his "functional" English made up of bits and pieces including some choice swear words he had acquired during his years in America. But he could read the sports section of the *San Francisco Chronicle*—the green section. Of course, he knew the game, was familiar with the players, could check the box scores and, amazingly, he could also follow the narrative reports of the games.

When I was seven or eight, I would pull out the sports sections of the old newspapers that father bought to wrap fish in. The papers went back a few years to 1928 or so when Babe Ruth was in his prime and I used to read about him and other players of the day. I spent hours doing that and wasn't much help in the store.

In 1932, when the Olympics were held in Los Angeles, the feats of the Japanese athletes were featured daily in the *Nichi Bei*, the Japanese vernacular paper that my father took. Japanese swimmers were especially dominant that Olympics and I remember reading about them in the Japanese section of the paper which was more detailed and more biased than in the English section.

At school when the magazine cart came around I always took "Boy's Life" and "Open Road for Boys," not for scouting or outdoor life which didn't interest me but for the sports stories. One boy in my class claimed he had read all the books in our school library. I was hardly his match but I was close. My subjects included classics, animal stories (dogs and horses), travel and

HIROSHI KASHIWAGI (RIGHT) AS BALTHAZAR, NATIVITY CYCLE. (UC BERKELEY, 1953 PHOTO BY RONALD PLOMGREN.)

exotic places, and of course sports. I wasn't too interested in folk tales, fantasies or science fiction. Sometimes I bought pulp westerns that were on display at Stevens Drug Store across the street from our store.

When I started to write in college, I began to pay special attention to the craft of writing, studying how other writers wrote and I developed an appreciation for writing. A well-written sentence is a joy to behold. Writing is not easy; it cannot be taught; perhaps it can be learned. I have taken quite a few classes in writing. Some were helpful, others were not. Camaraderie among the students is nice but unimportant. So too is criticism in the class; writers are primarily interested in their own work. I once had a professor, a distinguished writer himself, who was so critical of my work that I became discouraged and stopped writing completely. I think a writer, if he has any ability, should be encouraged, nurtured, even babied. There was a period of about ten years when I did not write at all. That was a very unhappy period of my life—a long dry spell. I think I was more irritable than usual, a bad husband and father. Encouraged by my family to satisfy my creative need, I took up leather craft, making leather hats, handbags, belts, etc. It was during the hippie period when leather and beads were in vogue. Not so now.

Then in 1975, I was discovered by two Sansei activists, Richard Wada and Doug Yamamoto, to whom I owe my new life as a writer. It was when Japanese Americans along with other minorities were trying to establish their identity. So I went to the shoeboxes where I kept my writings and pulled out the plays and stories. I rewrote the plays, many of which were written in the late forties and fifties, a more conservative time. The plays became more political, more straightforward in their messages and more Japanese American.

Ever since I had my first story published in a "little" magazine in Los Angeles, now long defunct, I had been writing stories and sending them out, hoping by chance to get accepted. No such luck. I had a few published in the Japanese American vernacular

SADAKO AND HIROSHI KASHIWAGI.

papers, usually in their holiday (Christmas and New Year) editions. While attending UCLA, I had a story published in *Scop*, a humor magazine. It was a literary story, hardly fit for a college humor magazine. To get around this the editors put in a somewhat risqué illustration which had little to do with my story.

My wife has suggested that the recovered plays be called "Shoebox Plays," which seems appropriate. At any rate, the Center for Japanese American Studies formed the Center Players to perform my plays and my friend Ted Samuel came on board as director. I have now known Ted, a graduate of Pasadena Playhouse, for over 50 years—ever since the late 40s when he directed my first play *The Plums Can Wait* with the Nisei Experimental Group in Los Angeles.

The Center Players was actually a family theater group consisting of five or six families, some of whose members were performers; others were curtain-pullers, sound and light people, costumers, supporters and morale-boosters. In our family, for example, I was the playwright and sometimes actor. My wife Sadako was a provider of refreshments at rehearsals and the official prompter during performances—very essential for the fledgling actors who were not accustomed to performing before an audience. Our middle son Soji, a tall teenager, pantomimed being a high-boy dresser on stage in the play *Laughter and False Teeth*, and the actors mimed getting their props from him. Our youngest son Hiroshi F. played Yoshio, the good boy, in the same play. We had a ready Japanese American audience who was interested in seeing their own stories enacted by Nikkei. After performing at various communities in the Bay Area, we traveled by chartered bus and performed at such places San Mateo, Union City, Merced, Stockton, Sebastopol. We even went to Los Angeles and performed at the old Union Church (now the new home of the East West Players) and at UCLA.

The Center commissioned me to write new plays for their Asilomar conferences and I wrote *Blessed Be*, *A Window for Aya*, and a play about our oldest son Tosh, who became disabled after being hit by a car while riding a bicycle.

As for my own acting, I have said that I started in Japanese Language School, which is true, but I think I really started in the public speaking class I took as a sophomore at Placer Union High School. When I got up on the riser, I became a totally different person, a "platform personality," which I learned to project on stage. I was told that I had a good speaking voice that I used to good effect. As I noted in the earlier pieces, I did considerable performing in camp. Then when we formed the Nisei Experimental Group in Los Angeles (1948-50) I learned some acting technique from the group director Hirotaka Okubo who generously shared what he had learned as an acting student at Los Angeles City College.

By necessity, acting has been an avocation for me since I had a full-time job as a professional librarian at San Francisco Public Library, though at one time I was a member of AFTRA (American Federation of Television and Radio Artists), SAG (Screen Actors

Guild), Actors Equity, and Dramatists Guild for playwriting. Currently, I retain membership in SAG and Dramatists Guild. Acting has been an "off-duty" activity. I often got calls from my agent at the library and once another staff member accused me of using the library as a casting agency.

On stage, I am proudest of my work in Philip Kan Gotanda's *The Wash* at the Eureka Theatre, San Francisco, when I performed with the late Nobu McCarthy. I was an understudy for the star Mako but when he could not do the part due to a film commitment, I was cast in the part. That's when I decided to retire from my library job, nine months short of my 65th birthday, in February 1987. I wanted to devote all my time to the rehearsals and performances and not feel guilty about "stealing" time from the library. To be honest, however, all my film and theater work was done during my off-duty hours.

On television, I am proud of my voice-over work in the antinuclear documentary *Dark Circle*. I was the English voice of an atomic bomb victim/survivor Taniguchi-san of Nagasaki. I also participated in Emiko Omori's *Hot Summer Winds*, in which I played a leader of a haiku poetry club and in her acclaimed documentary *Rabbit in the Moon*, about the resistance at Tule Lake Concentration Camp.

On film, there are two works worthy of mention—*Hito Hata: Raise the Banner*, the first Asian American feature film, in which I was privileged to work with Mako; and *Black Rain*, starring Michael Douglas in which I had a very small part as an actor playing a yakuza retainer (about 10 seconds on screen) which has been very lucrative for me; actually, it paid for a trip to Japan and back including all the omiage (gifts) I took my relatives and the souvenirs I brought back. Thanks to the popularity of the film, I have been receiving quarterly residuals for many years now though lately it has become a trickle. Every Sunday I still check the TV guide to see if *Black Rain* is playing anywhere.

Lately, I haven't heard from my agent; I wonder if he's still in business. When *Nash Bridges* was filming in San Francisco, I often got calls for extra work. This is mindless, boring work but I would take it because it was better than nothing, around $100 or better for 5 or 6 hours of work, mostly standing around and waiting. I have written about this work in another segment.

I have done quite a number of industrial videos. These are usually self improvement instructive videos made by companies for the benefit of their own employees. The industrials pay quite well though no meals are provided. On films, even for extras, time for lunch and often sumptuous catered lunches are provided, as required by the union. But industrials are difficult even for seasoned actors. The script is usually poorly written, crammed with information, often unrelated, and we are required to learn them in a short time.

Once for an industrial, after doing the two prepared scenes in the morning, the director brought me a completely new script, a one-page monologue that he asked me to learn during lunch. (We were given lunch in this instance—Chinese take-out.) Well, it was a monologue and I didn't have any interaction with another actor which made it easier. And it was quite well-written for a change. So, munching on chow mein, I learned the lines which came surprisingly easy. After lunch the director asked me if I could do it and I told him "Let's give it a try." I surprised myself and we were able to film the segment in one take—a whole page of monologue. That was satisfying.

I once did a commentary in English on how sake (Japanese rice wine) is made for the Takara Sake Factory in Berkeley. I was not a union member then and this was a non-union job for which I was paid $50. I know the commentary was used for many years in their tasting room. I was there once to check it out and told an official-looking person that I was the voice doing the commentary. I think I was given a small bottle of their sake—big payment for a modest service rendered.

My last job was another industrial I did for the Kaiser Permanente Hospital, an instructional video for new doctors on how to deal with terminally ill patients. Two years ago my agent called and told me he was looking for someone to play an Asian male in his 60s and asked me how old I was and I told him I was 78. "78?" he said, not believing me. When I told him indeed I was 78 he laughed and said, "I don't suppose you could play a man in his sixties." "Try me," I said. "Well...okay," he said and told me to show up for the audition. At the audition there were five other Asian males, all younger than myself, a couple I knew from previous auditions. I read with an actress who would eventually play the doctor opposite me. When we finished the audition the director thanked us and asked me how I felt about learning lines and I said "Okay," and that's when I had a feeling I got the part. My agent confirmed it a little later and sent me the script via e-mail. A week later the director called me at home to ask me how I was doing with the lines. He was concerned. I assured him that I had the lines "down," not to worry.

As for the shoot, I must say the hardest part was driving from San Francisco to the Kaiser headquarters in Oakland where the video was shot. I studied the map almost as hard as I did the script. The filming actually was a piece of cake, compared to the drive back to San Francisco without getting lost. Obviously, I am not a very confident driver. Recently, a doctor friend at Kaiser had seen me in the video and told me I looked very natural and young which was certainly good to hear. I was paid rather handsomely for the job but knowing that the video is appreciated and being used is a priceless reward.

Reading, writing, and acting—I have done all three for most of my life. I think I was born to act. However, when I was discouraged from pursuing an acting career, I turned to writing. I wanted to tell my story as well as the Japanese American story. But I could not abandon acting. So I joined my friend in Los Angeles to start our own theater group, which was to provide ourselves opportunities to act and to do theater. That's when I started to write plays, plays about ourselves and about events that were familiar to us. Usually, I would also write in an acting part for myself. I continued to read for pleasure, for content and edification, and for learning the craft of writing.

My personality has had a lot to do with my three pursuits. I, like many actors, am an introvert. I was extremely shy as a child and always quiet. I preferred to be alone, not exactly lonely, but alone. I have always found it awkward and difficult in social situation. My wife, who is more garrulous, has helped me a lot. I am not good at small talk. I have tried to overcome this and have done so to some extent. Acting has helped to bring me out of my shell. Notoriety as an actor and writer has also helped. So the solitary activities of reading and writing have come naturally to me.

But I am not an island unto myself. I need the contact with other people and I find this human relationship in reading, writing, and in acting. When I am reading I feel I am in communication with the writer. I know that the writer is speaking to me, sharing with me his or her thoughts, feelings, observations, experiences, and wisdom. I also have great respect for writers and their writings, how they write. On the other hand, when I am writing, I am writing for the reader, communicating with him or her and sharing the totality of myself. On the stage, I, as the actor, perform for the benefit of the audience but I need their response and participation. I can sense and feel their vibes and energy that drive my performance. Japanese American audiences, I'm sorry to say, tend to be less responsive, less animated, less vocal. They say it's a cultural thing but as an actor I think it's unfortunate, even cruel—there is no exciting theater, just frustrating hard work.

I have always liked sex but it's good only when it's happening. On the other hand, the so-called "high" that I get from reading, writing, and acting, is indescribable—so pleasurable, my bloodlife, my safety net, the world. Without them, there is no sun. That's it.

The Betrayed

by
Hiroshi Kashiwagi

PLACE:
ACT I: Tule Lake, an internment camp for Japanese and Japanese
    Americans during World War II
ACT II: Family room of Tak's house, Fresno, CA

TIME:
ACT I: February, 1943
ACT II: Late afternoon, early Summer, 1983

CHARACTERS:
Tak Fujimoto, ages 20 and 60
Grace Tamura, ages 20 and 60

*(The following information will be given to the audience before the
play begins.)*

During World War II, Japanese, aliens, and citizens alike, men,
women, and children, were removed from their homes on the
West Coast and imprisoned in the so-called Relocation Centers.
In February, 1943, the authorities ordered every evacuee 17 years
of age and older to register or answer a series of questions among
which were:

Question 27
Are you willing to serve in the armed forces of the United States
on combat duty wherever ordered?
Question 28
Will you swear unqualified allegiance to the United States of
America and faithfully defend the United States from any and all
attacks by foreign or domestic forces and forswear any form of
allegiance or obedience to the Japanese Emperor or any other
foreign government, power, or organization?

ACT I

SCENE 1

(*In the Ironing Room. Tak is standing by a table which serves as the ironing board. There is a wind-up phonograph to one side.*)

TAK: Grace, what're you doing?

GRACE: (*offstage R*) Locking the door.

TAK: Don't do that.

GRACE: (*entering*) Why not?

TAK: This is a public place.

GRACE: Oh, no one comes here to iron anyway, especially this late.

TAK: Then why are you locking the door?

GRACE: Just being careful; we don't want people barging in on us.

TAK: I still don't think it's right. I thought you were gonna iron aprons.

GRACE: I am and you're going to help me fold them.

TAK: (*noticing the phonograph*) What's that doing here?

GRACE: I don't know what you mean.

TAK: Don't pretend, Grace. The phonograph.

GRACE: Well, since you were doing so well last time, I thought we'd practice some more.

TAK: No.

GRACE: Why not?

TAK: I told you last time Grace, I'm not interested in dancing.

GRACE: That's a shame; you were just beginning to catch on; it could be fun. (*She starts to iron.*)

TAK: Hey, those are starched, aren't they? Why do you have to starch aprons?

GRACE: To make them look good. They're bleached too, you know.

TAK: Bleached?

GRACE: Yes. Don't they look nice, so white and clean? Doesn't it make you feel good wearing them?

TAK: What?

GRACE: Aprons, when you're working in the mess hall.

TAK: Oh I don't care.

GRACE: You don't care?

TAK: I just put it on…to protect my clothes I guess.

GRACE: Your jeans?

TAK: Yeah.

GRACE: No, you put the apron on to look clean and neat in the kitchen. So the diners won't see your grubby jeans.

TAK: Is that so? I didn't know that. *(beat)* Are you getting paid for doing this?

GRACE: No, I'm just helping my mother.

TAK: I'm surprised she's working as a washerwoman.

GRACE: My mother likes to wash; she used to do the hotel laundry. Besides, she's the only one with a washing machine. That's why they gave her the job.

TAK: *(after a moment)* We never had a washing machine.

GRACE: Oh? How did you do the wash then?

TAK: By hand; my mother did it by hand in the washtub on Sundays.

GRACE: That must have been quite a chore.

TAK: Well, we didn't change very often, maybe once a week.

GRACE: Once a week? Is that all?

TAK: Sometimes when I worked in the barn, I smelled like Grey, our horse.

GRACE: You smelled like a horse?

TAK: Have you ever stood ankle-deep in horse manure?

GRACE: What?

TAK: I mean with rubber boots on. I don't suppose you have. Not in Seattle. Well, I have. You want to hear about it?

GRACE: No.

TAK: Yes you do.

GRACE: I don't, really.

TAK: I'll tell you anyway. It feels kind of funny at first, you know, squishy and smelly. But when you start working, you know, shoveling the manure out the barn window, when you start getting into it, sweating and smelling like the barn, you begin to like the work. Yeah.

GRACE: Ugh.

TAK: And when you finish, when the barn's all clean, you feel clean yourself. You feel like you're part of the barn, like you belong there. And you feel close to the horse.

GRACE: I've been on a horse.

TAK: Oh yeah.

GRACE: My father used to take me to the park and put me on the carousel.

TAK: What's that?

GRACE: A merry-go-round.

TAK: Oh, a wooden horse.

GRACE: It must be scary to be near a…real horse.

TAK: Nah…well, you have to let it know when you come near it, especially from the back. Say "Whoa Grey" or "Whoa girl" or something like that. The horse knows your voice, you're friends. After all, you feed it, brush it, groom it.

GRACE: And clean out the…

TAK: Yeah. Just give it a slap on the rump and you can feel it quiver.

GRACE: Now that you've cleaned out the barn, I'd like to see it.

TAK: You would? I don't know about that. Nah, I can't picture you in the barn—chickens squawking, mice scurrying around...

GRACE: Mice?

TAK: Sure. A city girl like you in the barn...in high heels. (laughs)

GRACE: Don't be silly. I've been to a farm.

TAK: Oh? When?

GRACE: When we went on field trips. I remember seeing chickens and dogs and rabbits.

TAK: Yeah, that's quite a farm.

GRACE: (Goes to turn on the phonograph.) Would you like to practice? (Tak looks at her.) Come on, Tak. (He gives in.) Just give me a lead and I'll follow. That's right. Now, give me a strong lead, be decisive, decisive. That's it, you're doing fine. Don't stop now, Tak. Tak? (Tak stops in disgust.) You were doing fine. (He goes to turn off the music.)

TAK: I'm no dancer.

GRACE: Why didn't you learn?

TAK: Why should I? We lived ten miles out; we were bused in and dances were held after school, at nights mostly.

GRACE: You missed out on a lot of fun.

TAK: What're you talking about? I didn't miss out on anything.

GRACE: Didn't you want to go?

TAK: Hey, dances were for town kids, for hakujin.

GRACE: What did you do then?

TAK: I worked.

GRACE: At nights?

TAK: No, after school. By night I was tired; after a little home-work I went to bed.

GRACE: I worked too.

TAK: You're kidding me.

GRACE: No, I'm not.

TAK: I thought you were busy going to dances.

GRACE: I worked as a night clerk in the hotel.

TAK: What's that?

GRACE: I checked in guests...

TAK: Guests? Must have been a high class place.

GRACE: No, that's just a hotel expression; we even called bums guests.

TAK: Bums?

GRACE: Yes, we had a few sometimes and other transients—cannery workers, sailors...but most were permanent guests, people I've known all my life, godparents and aunties, they were like family to me. Miss Alice who taught me piano. Holidays were the best—Thanksgiving, Christmas, Easter—we celebrated together.

TAK: So what else did you do?

GRACE: Well, I gave out keys...but mostly I sat there.

TAK: Sounds like easy work.

GRACE: Well, somebody had to be there.

TAK: Like a watchdog, huh?

GRACE: Sort of. Had lots of time to study, read, listen to music. Oh, and I took messages too.

TAK: You mean telephone messages?

GRACE: Yes.

TAK: Oh yeah? *(beat)* I never used a telephone.

GRACE: You haven't? I can't believe it. I didn't know California was so primitive. Where did you say you were from?

TAK: Paradise.

GRACE: No running water.

TAK: Who said we didn't have running water? We had pipes inside.

GRACE: But no inside toilets.

TAK: No.

GRACE: And no telephones.

TAK: It's still a good place; I'd go back right now, if they'd let me.

GRACE: What did you do in an emergency?

TAK: Emergency?

GRACE: When someone got sick. Oh, I know, you rode Grey to fetch the doctor.

TAK: Grey's a workhorse, you don't ride a workhorse. Hey, we had cars in emergencies. Other times we waited until we saw the person at school or in town. Word got around fast enough. *(There's a loud knock at the door; both freeze, then Tak hurries R, unlocks and opens the door, looks out.)* I think it was the Warden. *(Closes the door.)* I'll leave it unlocked, okay? *(Grace nods.)*

GRACE: Do you have any friends outside?

TAK: *(indicating outside)* You mean the Warden?

GRACE: No, back home.

TAK: Not a one. What about you?

GRACE: I have quite a few friends. Those I grew up with, those I met at the university, and of course my family at the hotel.

TAK: And they write to you, I suppose.

GRACE: All the time; they keep me busy answering them.

TAK: I hope you tell them about the miserable conditions here.

GRACE: I tell them the truth.

TAK: Bet you doctor it up.

GRACE: What do you mean?

TAK: Did you tell 'em we have baloney every day and it's horse-meat?

GRACE: (beat) That's not true.

TAK: You didn't know?

GRACE: No.

TAK: And you've been eating baloney? (laughs)

GRACE: Ugh.

TAK: No more baloney sandwiches for you, I see. I hear apple butter's good. That's what the kids live on. (beat) Did you tell 'em about us?

GRACE: About us?

TAK: Yeah, you and me.

GRACE: Oh, they know I met someone in camp.

TAK: A country boy from California?

GRACE: Yes.

TAK: That's me...that we've become good friends?

GRACE: Well...

TAK: (suddenly) They'll drop you.

GRACE: Who?

TAK: Your friends outside.

GRACE: No, they won't.

TAK: They're hakujin, aren't they?

GRACE: Yes.

TAK: They'll forget you.

GRACE: But they're my friends.

TAK: Don't be too sure.

GRACE: Just because you don't have any friends, I mean outside.

TAK: Who needs them. *(beat)* I had a friend once. Paul.

GRACE: Oh?

TAK: He died. *(beat)*

GRACE: Well, what happened?

TAK: I guess I knew him best in grammar school. He kept wanting me to sit next to him and I kept wondering why. I didn't see him much after we got to high school. Paul was always crazy about airplanes and flying. Finally he learned to fly and joined the RAF. He was shot down over Germany; he died before the war even started here.

GRACE: *(Sprinkles water on apron; playfully sprinkles some on Tak.)*

TAK: Hey, cut that out.

GRACE: Don't you like showers?

TAK: What do you mean? Are you trying to tell me I should shower?

GRACE: Well...

TAK: Yes you are. *(laughs)* Oh I'd shower once in a while but you know, every time I do, I think about the bath we used to take back home. You know furo, Japanese tub bath. Have you ever been in a furo?

GRACE: Furo?

TAK: Oh, you've been missing something. It's nothing like the showers here in camp. We country folks don't like showers. It's so open, standing around naked in front of everybody. Why the other day I was in the shower and who do you think was there? My Japanese language teacher from back home. I was more embarrassed for him. He looked so vulnerable, you know, standing there in a fig leaf pose. *(He puts his hand over his groin.*) I didn't know whether to greet him or not; he never taught us shower etiquette. *(beat)* But you never get warm in a shower. Here, I'll take you to our furo. It's winter but you have on a yukata, you know the cotton robe. Inside it's dimly lit. Never mind the soot and the cobwebs—that's all part of the furo. Take off your yukata and hang it on a nail. Take the stool and sit. Now scoop some water from the tub and soap yourself and wash thoroughly. Before you step in the tub, try the water with your toes; if it's too hot, add a little cold water. But leave it a little hot. Now, slowly slide yourself into the tub; it might be a little hot at first but you'll get used to it. Now for a nice, long soak. Relaxing, isn't it? Careful you don't fall asleep. When you step out, you're like a lobster—all red and steaming and tingling. Dry yourself quickly, put your yukata back on and hurry into the house. There's no heat in the house, your room is like an icebox. Get into bed quickly, you don't want to cool off, and lie under a mountain of futon. Nice and warm, huh?

GRACE: Oh Tak...that was so real...I feel like I've taken a furo. *(He kisses her lightly and moves away; she gets up slowly and starts to fold a dish towel.)* Isn't it dull?

TAK: What?

GRACE: Dishwashing.

TAK: I don't think so. The work's over before I know it. I like the guys I work with; we're a team, we're fast and efficient. Besides, we get to eat before everyone else.

GRACE: Is that all you think about—eating?

TAK: We get hotcakes right off the griddle, not that soggy stuff you get on the metal platter. We get to eat as much as we want. Hey, eating's important here. Nourishment for the body.

GRACE: What about your brain?

TAK: What about it? My brain's okay.

GRACE: Don't you think it could use some exercise?

TAK: It gets enough exercise talking with you.

GRACE: You could do better.

TAK: Knock it off, Grace. You remind me of a hakujin, so pushy.

GRACE: Well...you don't have to waste your time here.

TAK: I want to do better; that's why I took the speech class.

GRACE: Oh yes. I thought you were the best speaker in the class.

TAK: Aw, you're just saying that.

GRACE: Honestly Tak, people like listening to you, what you say is interesting.

TAK: Stop it, Grace.

GRACE: I mean it; you should be working for the *Dispatch*.

TAK: And work with those smart college guys who think they're so special?

GRACE: Most of them have only been to college a year or so; they're all right once you get to know them.

TAK: Grace, how do you think I feel? I'm just a—

GRACE: A farm boy. Tak, you have to stop thinking like that. You do all right with me.

TAK: Well, we know each other.

GRACE: You see.

TAK: What could I do at the *Dispatch* anyway?

GRACE: You could write.

TAK: Write?

GRACE: You probably write better than the college guys on the staff. I'm always correcting their copy and I'm just a typist.

TAK: I bet you're the best one on the staff; you should be the editor; you'd be the editor if you were a male.

GRACE: Well...(*beat*) We could be working together.

TAK: Yeah but...

GRACE: Why not?

TAK: It's too close to the Ad building.

GRACE: What do you mean?

TAK: Isn't the *Dispatch* office across the fence?

GRACE: Yes but—

TAK: I don't feel right crossing the fence.

GRACE: I do it everyday; what's wrong with that?

TAK: Grace, what do you do there?

GRACE: I'm a typist for the *Dispatch.* I told you that.

TAK: People are suspicious of those who work across the fence.

GRACE: That's nonsense, Tak, and you know it.

TAK: Let's just drop the subject.

GRACE: Okay but I wouldn't want to be a pearl diver all my life.

TAK: A pearl diver?

GRACE: A dishwasher!

TAK: I'd rather be a dishwasher than a stool pigeon.

GRACE: *(beat)* You can't mean that.

TAK: Well, look at the *Dispatch.*

GRACE: What about the *Dispatch*?

TAK: Aren't you part of the Administration?

GRACE: The *Dispatch* is an autonomous paper.

TAK: Don't use big words on me.

GRACE: It means we're independent.

TAK: Independent of what? Look at what you print—nothing but directives and announcements. You're working for the Administration.

GRACE: Everyone's working for the Administration. As long as we live here and we're peaceful and law abiding, we're serving the Administration. So where do you get the idea we're stool pigeons? That's an awful thing to say.

TAK: I know.

GRACE: Then why did you?

TAK: Well, you work for a hakujin.

GRACE: It's a job; I only do what I'm told to do. *(beat)* Tak, is there something about me?

TAK: Well, sometimes you act like a hakujin.

GRACE: How?

TAK: You're confident; you're sure of yourself. You know you're an American.

GRACE: I am.

TAK: You act like you belong here.

GRACE: I do; don't you feel that way too?

TAK: I have to remind myself.

GRACE: That you're an American?

TAK: Yeah.

GRACE: I can't understand that. *(beat)* Oh I admit we print a lot of announcements but we try to make them clear and interesting. It isn't easy living here and we try to reflect that, but mostly we try to make it easier for everyone.

TAK: Okay Grace, I read the *Dispatch* every day.

GRACE: Do you find it interesting?

TAK: Well, you said it was about camp and camp's no picnic.

GRACE: How can we improve it?

TAK: What, the camp?

GRACE: No, the paper.

TAK: You can make up stories.

GRACE: You mean fiction?

TAK: I guess.

GRACE: Like *Little Women?*

TAK: Or like *Tom Sawyer.*

GRACE: *Heidi.*

TAK: *Robinson Crusoe.*

GRACE: *Secret Garden.*

TAK: *Northwest Passage.*

GRACE: *Black Beauty.*

TAK: *Moby Dick.*

GRACE: *Pride and Prejudice.*

TAK: *Last of the Mohicans.*

GRACE: *Wuthering Heights.*

TAK: *Call of the Wild.*

GRACE: You know, you have read a lot, Tak; when did you have the time?

TAK: Oh, on rainy days when we couldn't go out.

GRACE: Have you ever thought of going to college?

TAK: College? Nah.

GRACE: You should. You don't want to be a farm boy forever.

TAK: What's wrong with being a farm boy?

GRACE: Nothing, but you should widen your horizons and college can do that.

TAK: College was out of the question, my father being sick. But when they opened the student relocation here, I went to see about it.

GRACE: You did?

TAK: Even before I could sit down, they asked me if I had a thousand dollars.

GRACE: So?

TAK: So I left; I never had a thousand dollars in my life. Did you apply? I guess you didn't, you're still here.

GRACE: My father was in the detention camp at Santa Fe and I didn't know what was going to happen to him; I didn't want to leave my mother alone.

TAK: Oh yeah.

GRACE: Tak, why don't you try again?

TAK: What for, I don't have the money.

GRACE: Don't worry about the money. Now that my father's with us, I'll apply too. We'll go out together, okay?

TAK: You'd do that for me?

GRACE: Sure.

TAK: (*He goes to the phonograph, winds it and turns on the music.*) May I have this dance, Miss Tamura?

GRACE: Yes, Mr. Fujimoto.

TAK: (*He leads her expertly in the dance.*)

GRACE: Where did you learn to dance like this?

TAK: From you; you taught me, remember?

GRACE: (*Laughs, shakes her head as they dance.*)

(*Lights fade to darkness; end of scene.*)

SCENE 2

(*At the firebreak during a dust storm; both Grace and Tak are in heavy GI mackinaws with their collars turned up; Grace is wearing a kerchief. They are huddled close, trying to protect themselves from the dust swirling about them.*)

GRACE: What are we doing here?

TAK: Well, we're together and there's no one outside in this storm.

GRACE: Privacy at last.

TAK: Yeah, with a curtain of dust.

GRACE: I guess everyone's inside trying to keep out the dust, covering windows and plugging up holes. But it's no use, the sand comes through the walls and it'll be everywhere—on the beds, tables, chairs, windowsills, clothing...and gritty underfoot.

TAK: And in your eyes and nostrils too. (*He spits.*) Look at that—black. What a hellhole they put us in.

GRACE: I'd hate to go back now. Mother will be in tears and father will be cross.

TAK: Who can blame them? This is no place for humans.

GRACE: It's the best reason for wanting to leave.

TAK: Yeah.

GRACE: Tak, let's go outside.

TAK: We are outside.

GRACE: I mean out of here, out of this hellhole.

TAK: Grace, are you all right?

GRACE: Of course I'm all right. Why do you ask?

TAK: Well, it's hard to stay sane in these conditions.

GRACE: (*laughs*) I'm all right. Don't worry about me.

TAK: Remember, there's the fence and the soldier up in the guard tower with itchy fingers and a Jap near the fence would be a nice, easy target.

GRACE: I meant walk out through the front gate with the full blessings of the authorities. Then we'll be free, free to go anywhere we want.

TAK: You don't mean anywhere.

GRACE: Well, no. But out of here. Tak, if you want to go to college, you can.

TAK: Wait a minute Grace, are you talking about the registration?

GRACE: Yes, they're going to let us leave here; in fact, they want us to leave. That's why the questionnaire.

TAK: It's more complicated than that.

GRACE: How can it be? If we're loyal Americans, what's so hard about declaring it; that's what they want to know.

TAK: This storm, this hellhole, do you like it? Is this any way to treat Americans? I'm not going to sign anything just because they want me to.

GRACE: I didn't know you felt that way.

TAK: Well now you know.

GRACE: You're not one of those fanatics who are pro-Japan, are you?

TAK: No but I know some people who are.

GRACE: You do?

TAK: They have a right to feel that way. My uncle's one of them; his wife and children are in Japan. I try not to listen to him. *(There's a sudden gust of wind and both are nearly obscured by the dust.)* It's impossible to talk out here with all this dust.

GRACE: Tomorrow, why don't we meet at the *Dispatch* office?

TAK: I'm not comfortable there.

GRACE: No one will be there after work.

TAK: Yeah sure.

GRACE: I'll talk to Fred, tell him I'll be working late.

TAK: Who's Fred?

GRACE: Fred Williams, the Reports Officer.

TAK: Your boss?

GRACE: Sort of.

TAK: What about the gate? How will I get through?

GRACE: Here, take my pass; they know me so I won't need it.

TAK: I don't know about this...

GRACE: Oh come on, Tak. It'll be quiet there and...we'll be alone.

TAK: Alone?

GRACE: Yes.

TAK: I'll be there.

(*Lights dim to darkness.*)

SCENE 3

(*At the* Dispatch *office, late afternoon, next day. There's a knock and Grace lets Tak in. The room is furnished with a table, a couple of chairs and a bulletin board upstage. A typewriter is on the table.*)

TAK: Hey, there's something different about this place. What is it? (*Looks around.*) I smell an Englishman.

GRACE: Maybe Fred's English. Don't worry, he's not here, nobody's here. (*Tak goes around sniffing.*) Tak, you're like our dog.

TAK: You have a dog here?

GRACE: He belongs to Fred, a burly St. Bernard, gentle as a baby. He's our mascot. His name is—

TAK: Don't tell me. Tiny.

GRACE: How did you know?

TAK: Simple. Just like the *Dispatch*, no imagination. (*laughs*)

GRACE: Would you like some juice? I think we have some in the refrigerator.

TAK: How about a hamburger and milkshake.

GRACE: Sorry, the best I can do is coffee.

TAK: You gotta do better than that.

GRACE: Well then, let me see...how about canoeing?

TAK: Canoeing?

GRACE: Yes, on Lake Washington. (*She gets up on the table; motions him to join her; he climbs up.*) Easy, you're on a boat, remember.

TAK: Oh yeah...safe?

GRACE: I think so. Got your oar?

TAK: Uh huh.

GRACE: This is how you do it. *You go deep in the water, full paddle up, keeping your weight parallel to the water. Got it? (They paddle.) Yes, yes, now switch. (They switch.) This way you stay in a straight line. Yes. (They paddle switching. She spies something in the distance.) What's that?*

TAK: Where?

GRACE: Over there.

TAK: Ah...fish? *(Suddenly)* Invasion! The Rising Sun! *(They paddle frantically; Tak starts to fall, taking in water.)*

GRACE: Tak, get up. *(She helps him up.)*

TAK: You saved me, thank you.

GRACE: You're welcome. *(They paddle a bit more, then she puts out her hand. Tak realizes the ride is over, helps her down.)* Thanks for the ride.

TAK: Anytime. *(Grace exits L, returns with a glass of juice.)* Lots of space here.

GRACE: I'll give you a tour later; the lounge is back there. The editorial room is beyond Fred's office but I do most of my work here.

TAK: Did he write the registration order?

GRACE: Who, Fred? *(Tak nods.)* No, that came from Washington.

TAK: *(finishing his juice)* The mess crew and about twenty other guys in our block decided not to register.

GRACE: When did that happen?

TAK: Last night at our block meeting.

GRACE: And your decision?

TAK: To go along with them.

GRACE: How does your family feel?

TAK: My mother's worried, she wants to keep the family together. She depends on me...too much.

GRACE: And your father?

TAK: I don't know; he's in a hospital outside. He's leaving the decision up to me.

GRACE: You'll be going against orders, if you don't register.

TAK: I know.

GRACE: They can put you in jail.

TAK: Hey, we're already in jail.

GRACE: But they can put you in the stockade. You want to risk that?

TAK: I thought I'm an American.

GRACE: Yes, you are, you're loyal to your country and of course you'll defend it. That's all they want to know, why can't you tell them that?

TAK: Why should I?

GRACE: You're just making it difficult for yourself.

TAK: Grace, you're being so Japanese.

GRACE: You said I was too hakujin, now you're saying I'm too Japanese.

TAK: I mean you're so accommodating. When you used to go to your parties, your fancy hakujin parties that you talked about—

GRACE: What has that got to do with this?

TAK: I bet you brought the most expensive gift, I bet you were the best mannered and the most agreeable person there. And the ladies said, "Oh, you Japanese are so polite."

GRACE: What's wrong with being polite?

TAK: I bet you even stayed late to help clean up.

GRACE: Tak, you're a boor!

TAK: What's that?

GRACE: An animal! *(beat)* Tak, what's the matter with you?

TAK: There's a lot you don't know about me, Grace. I'll tell you something. When I used to ride the bus to school, there was this guy who would snap my ear from behind. Well, I looked straight ahead, never turned around, even though my ear was burning. I knew he wanted to start something and I wouldn't give him that satisfaction. But I was also afraid, afraid of the barrage of "Japs" that would rain on me if I did anything. I could feel the sting going away but inside I was sick and miserable because I had to take it.

GRACE: And refusing to register is your way of fighting back?

TAK: Yeah, for all the insults I've taken, for all the times I was called a Jap. *(beat)* Hey, it's a good feeling. I never knew it could be so good. *(voice rising)* It's liberating. Is that the right word Grace?

GRACE: Tak, be reasonable. Not registering is like saying "no" to the questions. You'll be labeled a "disloyal," you'll be put in jail or even sent to Japan. You don't want that, do you? Think about it, Tak.

TAK: I can only think of Howard.

GRACE: Howard?

TAK: Yeah, the bully who used to torment me. Every time he saw me, he would laugh at me. He had those long arms; one time when I was passing by, he socked me right in the chest. My chest ached for months; I thought it would never go away.

GRACE: Maybe he liked you?

TAK: Liked me?

GRACE: Have you ever thought of that?

TAK: How could he like me?

GRACE: People have strange ways of expressing themselves sometimes.

TAK: You mean hakujin?

GRACE: Not necessarily.

TAK: *(after a moment)* What are you gonna do...about the questions?

GRACE: My father's been after me to register.

TAK: But he was arrested by the FBI and held as a dangerous alien, why would he want you to register?

GRACE: He thinks it's the right thing to do; I've been making excuses and holding out.

TAK: Waiting for me?

GRACE: I've never gone against him.

TAK: Well, don't start now because I'm not going to register.

GRACE: Sometimes, I wish we had never met.

TAK: The camp brought us together...

GRACE: We're so different...what's going to happen to us?

TAK: I don't know.

GRACE: *(after a moment)* Let's pretend nothing's happening out there, let's pretend we're back in Seattle.

TAK: Yeah?

GRACE: You drive up in a car...

TAK: What car?

GRACE: You have to have a car to go on a date.

TAK: Oh yeah.

GRACE: We'll have dinner at a nice restaurant...let's see where could we go...ah, the Olympic Hotel.

TAK: Is that good?

GRACE: The best in Seattle.

TAK: (*In the restaurant, looking around*) Have you ever been here before?

GRACE: Yes, I come here every now and then. (*They sit.*)

TAK: Who's that guy in the funny suit?

GRACE: He's the waiter.

TAK: (*loudly*) I rather go to a drive-in movie.

GRACE: (*quieting him*) After our elegant dinner.

TAK: (*holding up a glass*) How about some wine?

GRACE: That's a water glass.

TAK: Oh...

GRACE: Besides, you'll need an ID to prove you're 21.

TAK: (*holding up Grace's pass*) I've got this pass that proves I'm you. (*He laughs as Grace takes the pass from him; they finish dinner.*)

GRACE: Wasn't that a lovely dinner?

TAK: It was okay. Now we'll get a hamburger after the movie. At the movie, we'll sit close together and I'll put my arm around you and tell you how beautiful you are. (*He kisses her; after a moment Grace breaks away.*) What's the matter?

GRACE: Nothing.

TAK: Did I do something wrong?

GRACE: No.

TAK: What is it, Grace?

GRACE: You know why they put us in camp, don't you? Because they didn't trust us. Well, the registration is a way out for us; it's a way we can prove we're good Americans.

TAK: We're not good Americans?

GRACE: They want proof.

TAK: Why do we have to prove ourselves over and over again? Aren't we good enough the way we are? I'm sick of saying yes, to everything. Yes, I'll go to camp. Yes, I'll register. Yes, I'll declare my loyalty. Yes, I'll serve in the Army and prove I'm a loyal, patriotic American.

GRACE: People are making a commitment to go to war and putting their lives on the line. It takes courage to make such a commitment.

TAK: I know it takes courage.

GRACE: Then why were you mocking it?

TAK: I wasn't mocking anything; I was just making a point. I'm proving my loyalty by fighting for my rights.

GRACE: Tak, how do you feel about the draft? You know the question asks if you're willing to serve in the Army.

TAK: I know what the questions ask. Grace, what are you driving at? That I'm trying to evade the draft, that I'm afraid of killing and dying, are you saying I'm a coward?

GRACE: No.

TAK: But you thought it. It's all right! *(in a gentler tone)* It's all right. Maybe you're right; I don't know, it's so mixed up. I know I don't like the idea of killing, never have.

GRACE: On that morning we left Seattle the residents fixed breakfast for mother and me...

TAK: To go to war, you have to be convinced it's right...

GRACE: and we all sat together and ate together.

TAK: there can't be any doubt, you can't even think about it...

GRACE: The table was beautifully set...

TAK: just march to the drumbeat.

GRACE: lace tablecloth, our best silver and chinaware, crystal.

TAK: I think I can be trained to be a soldier, learn to kill and be killed.

GRACE: They even had flowers and they played my favorite Baroque music.

TAK: Just listen to the drumbeat.

GRACE: I can almost hear it now. (*music in the background*)

TAK: On the day before we left, I slaughtered a flock of my Rhode Island reds I had raised from chicks. I didn't want to sell them and I didn't want to leave them...

GRACE: We didn't know when we would see each other again.

TAK: so I chopped off their heads. Blood spattered on my hands...

GRACE: They said they would be waiting for us.

TAK: I could feel the powerful struggle for life and I could feel that life going out.

GRACE: Now I'm not so sure.

TAK: (*to Grace*) I don't want to break with you; I don't want to do that. Grace, I love you.

GRACE: I love you too, Tak.

TAK: Let's close out everything...just you and me.

GRACE: And promise never to part.

TAK: Yes. (*They embrace and kiss; lights fade to darkness.*)

SCENE 4

(*Following night in the ironing room; Grace is ironing; there's a knock at the door and Tak enters. He's wearing a baseball cap and has a ball and a glove.*)

TAK: (*brightly*) Hi Grace.

GRACE: Is the game over already?

TAK: Yeah, we won, no thanks to me.

GRACE: What happened?

TAK: I misjudged a fly ball; it was so embarrassing; I could have died out there. (*moving toward Grace*) Wasn't that beautiful last night?

GRACE: Yes, it was.

TAK: It's the best thing that happened to me in camp. *(They kiss quickly.)*

GRACE: Remember the concert?

TAK: What concert?

GRACE: The classical record concert.

TAK: Oh yeah. But why are you bringing that up now?

GRACE: Well...it's where we first met.

TAK: Was it? I used to see you at softball games; you were with Mary...what's her name?

GRACE: Shimada.

TAK: I saw you cheering when I got a base hit.

GRACE: And laughing when you struck out.

TAK: Aw...

GRACE: What were you doing at the concert anyhow?

TAK: Didn't you expect to see me there?

GRACE: Frankly, no.

TAK: Why not? I hadn't heard much music before, maybe some hillbilly songs on the radio; I was curious about the classical stuff.

GRACE: I guess I was curious about you.

TAK: Say, I noticed that; you started talking to me right away. You told me you were taking a course in public speaking.

GRACE: And what do you know? You showed up the next night.

TAK: *(laughing)* Well, you made it sound so good.

GRACE: I learned a lot about you from your speeches.

TAK: I didn't know what to say; you all looked so smart.

GRACE: Did we?

TAK: Well, you spoke good English, using big words I never even heard before; some of you had fancy eyeglasses on.

GRACE: You told us about Grey and about your goat—how you had to milk it every day and how you hated the milk.

TAK: *(laughing)* That was Pinto.

GRACE: And how you were driving when you were nine years old.

TAK: Only on the back roads.

GRACE: That was two months ago.

TAK: And we've become good friends; it'll be great living in the country. You'll like it, Grace.

GRACE: Wait, Tak...

TAK: Do you like kids?

GRACE: What?

TAK: I love you Grace. *(He moves to kiss her.)*

GRACE: *(turning away)* Tak, I...

TAK: Grace...

GRACE: I have to be honest with you...

TAK: What is it?

GRACE: Tak, I can't see you anymore.

TAK: What?

GRACE: I'm sorry.

TAK: But last night...

GRACE: I know.

TAK: Grace, you can't do this to me. I love you.

GRACE: No, Tak.

TAK: You love me too. You said so last night.

GRACE: Yes, but...I can't, I just can't.

TAK: Why?

GRACE: I've decided to register.

TAK: (beat) But we agreed last night…

GRACE: Tak, I've thought about it again.

TAK: You're not being honest at all.

GRACE: No, Tak. If I don't register, I'd be going against myself, everything I believe in, everything that my father—

TAK: You've been talking to him again. Why do you do that?

GRACE: Because he's my father.

TAK: And you still think he's right.

GRACE: He's always been right.

TAK: Yeah, telling people to register, to volunteer for the Army.

GRACE: (overlapping) He believes in America right or wrong.

TAK: (overlapping) After what he went through, picked up by the FBI…

GRACE: (overlapping) All community leaders were taken…

TAK: (overlapping) And put in internment camps for enemy aliens…

GRACE: He was released.

TAK: Waving the American flag. With leaders like him, it's no wonder we're second class citizens.

GRACE: Tak, you don't know my father. He's always believed in America. That's why he went to school, took the trouble to learn English, worked and saved his money to invest in business, to start a new life here. He did this not only for himself but for his family, for me. He's always taught me to be an American, a good American.

TAK: Then why are we here?

GRACE: He always made me believe that there was a future here in America.

TAK: (louder) Grace, why are we here in camp?

GRACE: We were caught…in a war with Japan.

TAK: We were caught all right and put behind barbed wire.

GRACE: Someday the war will be over and we'll be out of here; there is a life after camp, you know.

TAK: Yeah, as second class citizens. Well, it's going to stop right now.

GRACE: What about the penalties for violating the Espionage Act—$10,000 or 20 years in prison or both?

TAK: That's stuff you guys at the *Dispatch* printed—all lies and threats to break down the resistance.

GRACE: Are you sure?

TAK: That's a chance I'll take.

GRACE: If you resist the registration, you'll be labeled a disloyal American. You don't want that hanging over your head the rest of your life, do you?

TAK: I'm defending my rights as a citizen. Does that make me disloyal?

GRACE: Tak, there's a future out there; if we do anything rash, we could jeopardize that future.

TAK: Grace, whose future are we talking about? Yours? Certainly not mine and not ours.

GRACE: I know we've been wronged, but I believe America will make it up to us. I trust my country.

TAK: You mean you trust your father.

GRACE: Leave my father out of this.

TAK: Then what about the promise we made last night? What about it, Grace?

GRACE: Oh Tak...

TAK: I knew it was too good to be true. (*Lights down then up on Tak at DR.*) Back in kindergarten when I could barely speak English, I learned the Pledge of Allegiance from a teacher who came every morning riding a horse. Good Morning, Children.

Good Morning, Miss Moore. We recited the Pledge of Allegiance every morning at the beginning of school. Through the years I've recited it thousands of times. *(Lights up on Grace as they both recite the pledge.)*

Both: I pledge allegiance to the flag of the United States of America and to the Republic for which it stands, one Nation, indivisible, with liberty and justice for all.

(Lights dim to darkness.)

END OF ACT I

ACT II

SCENE 1

(Forty years later, 1983, Fresno, California. In the family room of Tak's house; the room is simply furnished with some chairs, a footrest, a coffee table and a Buddhist shrine. There is a tape deck at UL and a bar at UR. A Japanese scroll hangs on the wall at UC. It is late afternoon. Grace is settling down in a chair when Tak enters with two mugs of coffee.)

TAK: You'll have to take it black; I'm all out of cream.

GRACE: That's fine.

TAK: Good. I guess I don't do much cooking around here.

GRACE: I'm sorry to put you to trouble.

TAK: No, it's no trouble.

GRACE: *(Referring to the photo on the shrine.)* Is that your son?

TAK: Yeah, Tommy. *(An awkward moment.)*

GRACE: I'm sorry.

TAK: Maybe later.

GRACE: Surprised to see me?

TAK: Well, you never know who'll show up at a camp reunion.

GRACE: I thought you might be registered.

TAK: Registered?

GRACE: Something wrong?

TAK: No, it's just the word; I hadn't heard it in years. I'm sorry, you were saying...

GRACE: I thought surely you'd be at the reunion, you live right here in Fresno. I came all the way from Chicago.

TAK: Well, reunions...

GRACE: Actually, I came for the redress campaign.

TAK: That's right, you told me on the phone.

GRACE: I understand you're not involved.

TAK: No, I'm not.

GRACE: Why not, Tak?

TAK: Well, the farms take up a lot of my time and...

GRACE: Guess I'll have to convince you how important this is.

TAK: Is that why you showed up all of a sudden?

GRACE: We need all the support we can get.

TAK: Here I thought you came to see me.

GRACE: Well, I hoped I could see you.

TAK: Is that right?

GRACE: I knew there was a good chance of seeing you.

TAK: I've often wondered about you.

GRACE: It's been a long time.

TAK: Yeah.

GRACE: Well, I didn't come to talk about the past.

TAK: Yeah...hey, you're looking great.

GRACE: Thanks.

TAK: You were always sophisticated but now you're a little bit more.

GRACE: Yes, a little bit more. *(She indicates her hips.)*

TAK: I didn't mean that. You have class, Grace, foxy as the kids say.

GRACE: Oh, stop that.

TAK: You really haven't changed much, Grace.

GRACE: Oh, I have. After all it's been forty years and a lot of living —marriage, children...

TAK: How many?

GRACE: Two daughters and three grandchildren. And you?

TAK: A boy and a girl, their kids...let's see *(counts mentally)* five I guess.

GRACE: Five grandchildren! You and your wife must be proud.

TAK: My ex-wife.

GRACE: Oh yes.

TAK: And you're a widow.

GRACE: *(nods)*

TAK: *(smiles)*

GRACE: Is there something?

TAK: Well, I was just thinking...you could have been my wife.

GRACE: Oh, stop that.

TAK: You're into some kind of writing?

GRACE: I'm an editor for a publishing house. *(Shows him her card.)*

TAK: I'm impressed.

GRACE: It's only a small company.

TAK: You've done all right for yourself; remember how I told you in camp you should be the editor of the *Dispatch*? Remember that?

GRACE: Yes, I do. You haven't changed much yourself, Tak.

TAK: (pointing to his head) All gray.

GRACE: (startled) Gray?

TAK: Something wrong?

GRACE: No. It's just that when you said "gray" I was reminded of the horse; you know the one you used to talk about so much?

TAK: Oh yeah, I remember.

GRACE: You certainly told me a lot about her.

TAK: (laughs) Good ole Grey. I heard she was replaced by a ranch truck during the war. I never did see her again. We didn't go back to Paradise, you know.

GRACE: You settled here in Fresno after camp?

TAK: Yeah. We worked as farm laborers for five years—my mother, my brother and I and we saved enough to buy our first ranch.

GRACE: And your father was still in the hospital?

TAK: Yeah. Once we brought him home for a visit. He stayed a week. You know, he just couldn't stay still; he had to go out- side and walk around the ranch, get a feel of it. He always wanted a place of his own. I think we made him happy. (beat) He died soon after that.

GRACE: Now you're a famous man, a powerful farm leader. I read about you all the time.

TAK: Do you?

GRACE: Yes, even in the Chicago Tribune.

TAK: Chicago Tribune, heh? Well, I'm still a farmer with mud on my shoes.

GRACE: President of the Farmers League.

TAK: Yeah, twelve years.

GRACE: That long?

TAK: They won't let me quit.

GRACE: That was some achievement holding back the union.

TAK: We had to. If we let them push us out, we're gone. The corporations would have moved in. We're all small to mid-sized, independent farmers. We've lived and worked on the farms for twenty, thirty years. They thought they could run us out. They didn't know how tough we could be. Hell, we surprised even ourselves. We organized, closed ranks.

GRACE: Who would have thought that you, Tak, would be fighting the union?

TAK: What do you mean?

GRACE: Well, you said you worked for five years.

TAK: That's what I said; I've been a worker all my life. Look at my hands—these are working man's hands.

GRACE: Then what about your workers now?

TAK: What about them?

GRACE: Aren't they the victims?

TAK: Say, whose side are you on?

GRACE: Workers have their rights, you know, good working conditions and wages they can live on.

TAK: They get decent wages; it's not like when I was working; we take good care of our workers.

GRACE: What about housing and health care and education for the—

TAK: We do what we can; we don't run a welfare agency.

GRACE: Aren't the workers Mexicans?

TAK: I know what you're driving at. Hey, we run a business, we take risks, it's always a gamble for us. We can't be worried about people's nationality or race. The bottom line is—

GRACE: Profits!

TAK: Grace, you remind me of those young people marching in picket lines, waving placards, looking good on TV, young liberals who never did a lick of work in their lives.

GRACE: You're wrong, Tak, you're very wrong. Ever since the children were old enough to go to school, I've been in the work force. I helped raise our two daughters. After Herb died I've been on my own. I started as a file clerk and worked my way up in the company. I've paid my dues. I know what it means to be a worker.

TAK: I see we've come a long way.

GRACE: Yes, we have.

TAK: Who would have thought that you, Grace, would be defending the workers.

GRACE: (Starts to fidget and Tak looks at her curiously.)

TAK: Can I get you something?

GRACE: No. Around about now, I get a craving for a cigarette.

TAK: Oh, go right ahead. (He goes looking for an ashtray at the bar.)

GRACE: It's all right.

TAK: I used to smoke; I quit when our first child was conceived, you know when all that talk about cancer first came out.

GRACE: I quit too after my husband died.

TAK: Oh.

GRACE: Actually I had started in self-defense; he was a heavy smoker; smoking took the place of talking; it filled up space.

TAK: You mean you didn't talk?

GRACE: (Taken aback)

TAK: I'm sorry, that was dumb.

GRACE: It's all right; we had our problems…as in most marriages.

TAK: How long has it been since your husband died?

GRACE: Five years. By the way, thanks for the telegram you sent me.

TAK: You already thanked me in your letter.

GRACE: It meant a lot. *(beat)* How did you know about Herb's death?

TAK: I saw it in the *Pacific Citizen.*

GRACE: Oh? I didn't think you were a member of the JACL.

TAK: I'm not. Remember, they disowned us No-No's. Yeah, the Japanese American Citizens League. *(beat)* I suppose you're a member.

GRACE: Yes, I've been for a long time; lately, I've been working with their redress movement.

TAK: Oh yeah.

GRACE: Tak, I'm sure you have a lot of influence, especially among the farmers...

TAK: Well...I'm kind of busy.

GRACE: This is important to all of us.

TAK: Camp was a long time ago.

GRACE: I know it was.

TAK: Why bring it up now?

GRACE: Why not bring it up?

TAK: We're doing all right. Leave well enough alone, I'd say. It was painful enough when we lived through it.

GRACE: Yes, we all suffered; but unless we make our feelings known, nobody will know or even care about what happened to us.

TAK: Why are you saying this now?

GRACE: Tak, we didn't do anything wrong; it was the government that treated us like criminals.

TAK: Hey, Grace, you have changed.

GRACE: I thought you said I hadn't changed.

TAK: I mean your attitude towards the government.

GRACE: I felt this way in camp.

TAK: Did you? Then why did we break up?

GRACE: Please, Tak...

TAK: Or was it your father?

GRACE: What about my father?

TAK: He was pro-America; he tried to influence others and you listened to him.

GRACE: Why do you blame him?

TAK: Because he broke us up.

GRACE: No, Tak, believe me, it was my decision.

TAK: To break our promise?

GRACE: Tak, that was forty years ago.

TAK: I know it was. *(beat)* What happened to your father?

GRACE: He's gone now, died a few years ago.

TAK: I mean after camp.

GRACE: He resettled in the east.

TAK: Didn't he go back to Seattle?

GRACE: He did once.

TAK: What happened?

GRACE: He decided to live in the east. *(She looks at the photo on the altar.)* How did your son die?

TAK: Vietnam.

GRACE: Oh...

TAK: I feel like a drink; would you care for something, wine?

GRACE: No, thank you.

TAK: *(holding up his hand)* I'm supposed to ask you three times.

GRACE: Oh? And I'm supposed to refuse?

TAK: Yeah, even if you're dying for a drink. Are you? *(laughs)*

Mrs. Mori, would you care for something to drink?

GRACE: No, thank you, Mr. Fujimoto.

TAK: Are you sure now?

GRACE: Quite.

TAK: But I insist you join me in a drink.

GRACE: In that case, would you have any sherry?

TAK: Ah, sherry. I think I might have some sherry. *(He goes to the bar to fix the drinks; Grace meanwhile looks at the shrine. Tak returns with the drinks.)*

GRACE: He looked like you, Tak.

TAK: People always said that. *(He goes to the shrine and lights the candle and a stick of incense.)* He always had lots of friends, mainly hakujin.

GRACE: Oh? Did you encourage that?

TAK: I didn't; maybe Yuri did. Anyway, he was a friendly kid.

GRACE: You were close to him?

TAK: Yeah. I suppose I was closer to him than to the others. He was a natural athlete—basketball, baseball—it was a joy to watch him play; I could almost see him now. He always made the right moves.

GRACE: Did he?

TAK: I guess he didn't know what to make of us—Yuri and me.

GRACE: What do you mean?

TAK: Once he asked me why I hadn't been in the Army.

GRACE: Did you tell him about camp?

TAK: I tried to…then my wife started making excuses for me and I got angry at her…in front of Tommy. *(He takes a drink.)* He started college when I was busiest with my work—the farm, the work with the league. I didn't see him much and I guess we lost touch. *(beat)* Then one day he said he was volunteering for the Army. I told him he didn't have to do that; he could wait till he was drafted but he wouldn't listen to me. I suspected he was talking with my wife.

GRACE: What camp was your wife in?

TAK: She never went to camp; she comes from Colorado. Her family moved out here after the war.

GRACE: Did she know you were a No-no?

TAK: I told her... *(beat)* she said it didn't matter.

GRACE: But it did.

TAK: Yeah. Sometimes I wonder why we married. We never talked about camp. Can you imagine being married for thirty years, living together, eating together, sleeping together, making love and not talking about a certain subject? *(He goes to the shrine and strikes the bell.)* By the time Tommy was killed in action, our marriage was over. *(strike)* My son was ashamed of me, he was ashamed of me! *(beat)* He died trying to clear my name. *(He strikes the bell again.)*

GRACE: I don't know what to say.

TAK: There's nothing to say. *(beat)* Grace, have you ever thought about how it might have been if we had gone out of camp together?

GRACE: I have on occasion.

TAK: Maybe we would have gone to college together. You were always on me about that. *(Grace smiles.)* I would have gone to war. *(Carried away by the thought)* Yeah, I would have dodged bullets to prove my loyalty on the battlefield and come home a war hero with medals on my chest only to find that the battle had just begun. *(Tak is unaware that he is upsetting Grace.)* If I had returned a whole man, a miracle in itself, it would take more than a miracle to stay whole.

GRACE: Stop it, Tak! Stop it please!

TAK: Are you all right, Grace?

GRACE: I'm sorry...it's just that what you said was so close to home.

TAK: I didn't mean to upset you.

GRACE: I'm all right now.

TAK: So he was a war hero?

GRACE: Yes, with the 442nd Battalion.

TAK: You want to talk about it.

GRACE: I was taken with Herb's war record though he hated to talk about it. He just said he was lucky to be alive. *(beat)* We met at Northwestern when he was a GI student and I was working at the campus bookstore. We were married after he was graduated. He was an accountant, a good one but whenever it came time for a promotion, he was passed over.

TAK: Even as a veteran?

GRACE: *(nods)* Golf was his passion.

TAK: So you were a golf widow?

GRACE: Well, he had a heart attack on the golf course...

TAK: Oh, I'm sorry.

GRACE: He died doing what he loved to do; I've always been a golf widow.

TAK: And you didn't mind?

GRACE: No. *(Tak nods.)* The high point of his life, aside from his military years, was joining the country club. It took some doing.

TAK: More discrimination?

GRACE: Yes. He went about it like it was another war. My husband was a man who risked his life over and over again to prove his loyalty only to come back to a country that couldn't tell the difference between him—a war hero—and the enemy.

TAK: And you stuck by him?

GRACE: I didn't want him to stop believing that he had made a difference.

TAK: He did make a difference.

GRACE: What?

TAK: He made a difference for all of us.

GRACE: You really mean that, don't you?

TAK: Of course I do.

GRACE: You were a No-no.

TAK: Yeah, I made my statement forty years ago when I resisted the registration order and I was called a disloyal American. It wasn't popular but I did it because I had to. Everyone does what he has to do; your husband did what he did and I respect him for it.

GRACE: I'm glad to hear you say that, Tak.

TAK: Yeah, and Tommy did what he had to do. (*beat*) What hurts is that being a No-no I feel responsible for what he did.

GRACE: But you blamed your wife.

TAK: No, I was responsible; I should have made Tommy understand.

GRACE: That wasn't easy.

TAK: But Tommy's dead, I should have...

GRACE: Oh Tak...I wish there's something I could...

TAK: Yeah, I know. (*Tak indicates empty glass, Grace nods and he takes it to refill.*)

GRACE: (*Notices the footrest by the chair where Tak was sitting.*) That's quite an interesting footrest.

TAK: You like it?

GRACE: Yes.

TAK: I made it for the furo.

GRACE: Furo?

TAK: Yeah.

GRACE: I still remember the furo you described for me once; it was so sensual; you disrobed me and put me in the tub.

TAK: *(Embarrassed)* No, did I do that?

GRACE: Of course, it was all imaginary.

TAK: Yeah, imaginary…wow. But I must have told you to wash yourself first; that's the first thing. *(demonstrating)* You sit on this stool and wash yourself well before you step in the tub.

GRACE: *(Laughing)* Of course you did, I just forgot. Do you have a furo now?

TAK: No, not any more. We used to at the old house when my mother was still living.

GRACE: Then you don't take furo now?

TAK: Who has time? I shower.

GRACE: But I thought you hated showering.

TAK: That was in camp.

GRACE: *(beat)* Remember how we used to look for places to be alone—in the shadow of a barrack, in the firebreak during a dust storm, remember that? And in the ironing room?

TAK: Yeah, the ironing room.

GRACE: Remember how I used to iron aprons and dish towels so we could be alone in there?

TAK: Yeah, we got away with a lot too; the warden knew what we were up to but he looked the other way. Once you even locked the door.

GRACE: I did not.

TAK: Yes, you did. I distinctly remember it; it was a bold move, Grace.

GRACE: *(Embarrassed)* I don't remember that at all.

TAK: Oh come on. Once you even had me go to the *Dispatch*

office when everyone had gone home. There we were—all alone in the office where you people printed all that propaganda that caused so much trouble in camp—and we made love. Remember that?

GRACE: Yes, I do.

TAK: I've never forgotten it—the one beautiful moment in all that turmoil.

GRACE: It's like a jewel in my memory.

TAK: Like a jewel, huh? (beat) Grace?

GRACE: Yes?

TAK: I wish we could go back to that time.

GRACE: Don't be silly.

TAK: Why not?

GRACE: And relive all those unhappy days?

TAK: We had some good times.

GRACE: No.

TAK: What about now then? (They look at each other.) Even after all these years...

GRACE: (remembering) Please, Tak!

TAK: What's wrong, Grace?

GRACE: Tak, do you remember when you and the others from Block 42 were rounded up?

TAK: Why do you bring that up?

GRACE: Because you don't know what really happened.

TAK: It was February 21st, 1943. Thirty-five of us who had refused to register were taken to the stockade at bayonet point.

GRACE: (as though blaming Tak) Do you know what happened to us?

TAK: I heard you left camp soon after.

GRACE: Yes, for our safety.

TAK: What happened?

GRACE: The night after you were taken in, my father was walking home when he was chased by a gang of hoodlums. They caught up with him just as he got to our apartment so father sat down on the stoop and dared them to kill him. They left but only after they had spat on him, called him an America lover, a collaborator, an inu!

TAK: I'm sorry.

GRACE: Can you imagine how frightening that was? (*Tak shakes his head.*) After that we couldn't stay in camp. My boss at the *Dispatch* arranged an Army escort for us and we hurriedly packed some clothes and left the following night.

TAK: (*defensively*) I was in the stockade, I didn't know.

GRACE: My father never got over it; he didn't seem to care anymore. (*beat*) He lost his hotels, you know.

TAK: I didn't know that.

GRACE: They were in such bad shape, hardly worth the taxes he had to pay, so he sold them all, at a loss of course.

TAK: But with the housing shortage at the time surely he could have—

GRACE: I tried to tell him that.

TAK: What happened to him? He was always an entrepreneur.

GRACE: He spent the rest of his life as a caretaker of an estate.

TAK: Your father did that?

GRACE: Yes.

TAK: Why?

GRACE: He was looking for peace of mind.

TAK: And did he find it? Was he happy?

GRACE: I don't know. He never let on to me but mother told me he was miserable.

TAK: You said he went back to Seattle.

GRACE: Yes.

TAK: Your father believed in America, right or wrong?

GRACE: Don't, Tak, my father is dead.

TAK: Maybe he went too far.

GRACE: No.

TAK: What happened in Seattle, Grace?

GRACE: He was their leader, their advisor, their confidant; he represented them in court, wrote letters for them, helped them with business problems, gave them housing, found them jobs, took them to doctors, even brought them food when they were hungry. Yet...when he went back to Seattle after the war and tried to contact them, no one would speak to him, not even say hello.

TAK: Can you blame them?

GRACE: What?

TAK: After what he did in camp.

GRACE: Tak!

TAK: *(beat)* You know, Grace, I was warned not to associate with you in camp.

GRACE: Because of my father? *(Tak nods.)* Why didn't you tell me?

TAK: I knew how you felt about your father.

GRACE: All the more you should have told me.

TAK: I didn't want to hurt you.

GRACE: You weren't being honest.

TAK: You should talk.

GRACE: So you tried to spare me.

TAK: (*Before going to freshen his drink.*) How are you doing—your drink?

GRACE: (*irritated*) I'm all right!

TAK: Okay. (*going to the bar*) Forty years later and we're still talking about camp and the stupid registration. Isn't it about time we dropped the subject? And it wasn't even necessary.

GRACE: What wasn't necessary?

TAK: The registration.

GRACE: What do you mean?

TAK: We didn't have to register.

GRACE: (*after a moment*) You mean we didn't have to...

TAK: (*shakes his head*) Didn't you know?

GRACE: No!

TAK: Not many did, I guess; the authorities kept it from us—to save face.

GRACE: How do you know?

TAK: I read it in a book about camp years after I came out.

GRACE: And I'm in the book business.

TAK: (*laughing*) That's right.

GRACE: But why are you telling me now?

TAK: I thought you knew.

GRACE: (*suddenly*) Oh, Tak...I don't know what to think. I feel a cold wind...all those years...all those years...(*She begins to wail.*)

TAK: Don't, Grace.

GRACE: All those years.

TAK: Don't discredit those years.

GRACE: Oh, my life...(*She continues to wail; Tak comforts her and slowly she recovers.*) I was a perfectly loyal person, wasn't I? A loyal American doing exactly as my father, a super patriot, wanted me to. I did, thinking I had to. *(beat)* Then I married a man who fought in the war, another patriot. It served me right to have lived with ghosts all these years.

TAK: Ghosts?

GRACE: Yes, ghosts that haunted and tormented my husband! All those nightmares...

TAK: Nightmares?

GRACE: Yes, nightmares. *(suddenly)* Stop it, Herb! The war is over, can't you understand that?

TAK: Grace, Grace...

GRACE: You keep calling your buddies every night. I can't stand it anymore.

TAK: What're you saying, Grace?

GRACE: Why didn't you die with them, why didn't you die in Europe? *(sobbing)*

TAK: *(He takes hold of her.)* Grace, it's all right.

GRACE: *(Slowly returning to her senses.)* No.

TAK: But it's over.

GRACE: Is it?

TAK: Oh, Grace. *(He reaches for her and Grace turns away.)*

GRACE: *(beat)* Tak...

TAK: What is it, Grace?

GRACE: That promise we once made...

TAK: Yeah?

GRACE: I'm sorry, Tak.

TAK: Oh, Grace.

GRACE: Will you forgive me?

TAK: Grace, it's all right. *(They embrace.)*

GRACE: The banquet…I better get ready to go.

TAK: What's your hurry; there's plenty of time. Let's sit a minute, here by this window. (*He places two chairs at downstage center. Both sit and look out.*) What do you see, Grace?

GRACE: (*puzzled*) I don't understand…

TAK: Tell me what you see?

GRACE: Well…the sunset…

TAK: Uh huh…

GRACE: It's beautiful.

TAK: My mother used to sit here everyday around this time; bathed in the soft glow of the sun, I often wondered what she was doing?

GRACE: Maybe she was reliving her life.

TAK: Yeah, I think you're right, Grace. She seemed so happy.

GRACE: What do you see, Tak?

TAK: You mean out there?

GRACE: Yes, out there.

TAK: Well…(*he pantomimes looking through binoculars*) I'll be darned, I see…two lovers walking hand in hand. Yeah, and what do you know, one's an attractive woman who looks just like you, Grace.

GRACE: (*laughing*) And the other?

TAK: The other's an old farmer, gray-haired, but he looks to be in pretty good shape. (*They laugh and Tak takes her hand.*)

GRACE: (*beat*) Will you come with me to the reunion banquet?

TAK: Are you sure? I'm still a No-no, you know.

GRACE: My daughters think the No-no's were the real heroes and I agree.

TAK: Oh well, thanks…but I'm no hero. I'm just a country boy from Paradise, California.

GRACE: (*overlapping*) Paradise, California. I'd like you to come as my guest.

TAK: That should raise some eyebrows, especially here in Fresno.

GRACE: I'll risk it. I'll go freshen up. (*She starts to leave, then stops.*) About the redress...I hope you'll change your mind.

TAK: Well...I'll see what I can do with those farmers—yeah, with those hard-headed farmers.

GRACE: Thanks, Tak, thanks. (*She exits.*)

TAK: (*He starts to look through his tape collection, finds the one he wants, puts it on. It is "At Last," the song they used to dance to in camp. Grace returns, looking fresh and youthful.*) Remember this?

GRACE: Yes. (*They dance.*) You do pretty well, don't you?

TAK: Guess who taught me.

GRACE: You were the awkward country boy who didn't care to dance.

TAK: That's not how I remember it. (*They laugh and as they continue to dance, the lights fade to dark.*)

END OF PLAY